BOROUGH OF KEIGHLEY
PUBLIC LIBRARIES

REFERENCE LIBRARY

Book No	Class No.
18923	942.74

Books obtained for reference must not under any circumstances be taken from the Reference Library.

Works which are of special character and rarity, will be issued only on written application to the Chief Librarian.

The tracing of illustrations is prohibited.

Any person found writing, marking or otherwise mutilating any Book, Pamphlet, Manuscript Microfilm, Map, or periodical, will be proceeded against in accordance with the Library Bye-laws.

Books must be returned to the staff after consultation.

FRED TAYLOR, F.L.A.
Chief Librarian

May 1969

BRADFORD

Other Books in the Local History Series

BIRMINGHAM
John Sanders

THE BLACK COUNTRY
Edward Chitham

CANTERBURY
Marcus Crouch

CHESTER AND THE NORTHERN MARCHES
Guy Williams

CHICHESTER AND LEWES
Barbara Willard

EDINBURGH
Hugh Douglas

GLOUCESTER, STROUD AND BERKELEY
Edward Hayward

LIVERPOOL
Mary Cathcart Borer

SHREWSBURY AND SHROPSHIRE
Dorothy P. H. Wrenn

YORK
Peter Wenham

BRADFORD

Joseph Fieldhouse

Illustrated by Paul Shardlow

Longman

LONGMAN GROUP LIMITED

LONDON

Associated companies, branches and
representatives throughout the world

Text copyright © Joseph Fieldhouse 1972

Illustrations copyright © Longman Young Books 1972

First published 1972

ISBN 0 582 15079 5

*Printed in Great Britain by
Clarke, Doble & Brendon Ltd
Plymouth*

ACKNOWLEDGEMENTS

The author wishes to thank the following for their co-operation in making information available to him:

The Director, Bradford City Art Gallery and Museums; the Town Clerk, City of Bradford; the City Development Officer; the Secretary, Bradford Community Relations Council, and the Editor-in-Chief, *Bradford Telegraph and Argus*.

The author and publishers would like to thank the following for permission to use copyright material:

Cambridge University Press *Place Names of the West Riding of Yorkshire* Smith, A. W. (p. 20)

Pitman Press *The Story of Bradford Law*, M.C.D. (p. 72)

Bradford City Librarian *Abraham Balme's Diary* (MS) (p. 76) and *Empsall Papers* (MS) (pp. 121–2)

Chairman, City of Bradford Educational Services Committee *Education in Bradford since 1870* (p. 167)

FURTHER READING

CUDWORTH, W., *Round About Bradford*. (Reissue, Mountain Press, 1968.)

GILL, J. C., *Parson Bull of Byerley*. (SPCK, 1963.)

HEATON, H., *The Yorkshire Woollen and Worsted Industries*. (2nd ed., Oxford Clarendon, 1965).

JAMES, J., *The History and Topography of Bradford*. (Reissue, Mountain Press, 1967.)

MANSBRIDGE, A., *Margaret McMillan*. (Dent, 1932.)

PIKE, E. R., *Human Documents of the Industrial Revolution*. (Allen & Unwin, 1966.)

ROWE, J. H., *The Book of Bradford*. (Brocklehurst, 1924.)

SCRUTON, W., *Pen and Pencil Pictures of Old Bradford*. (Reissue, Mountain Press, 1968.)

SIGSWORTH, E. M., *Black Dyke Mills*. (Liverpool University Press, 1958.)

SIMPSON, A. E., *A Short History of Bradford Cathedral*. (British Publishing Company, 1964.)

Education in Bradford, 1870–1970. (Bradford Corporation, 1970.)

The Centenary Book of Bradford, 1847–1947, (Byles, 1947).

CONTENTS

Chapter   **Page**

1.   Bradford up to the Norman Conquest   11

2.   The De Lacys, the Plantagenets and the Boar Legend   25

3.   Bradford Before the Civil War   43

4.   The Civil War and its Aftermath   51

5.   Eighteenth-century Wool Trade and the Bradford Canal   66

6.   On the Verge of the Industrial Revolution   78

7.   Early Days of the Industrial Revolution   90

8.   "Yorkshire Slavery" and Riots   101

9.   Expanding Trade and the Railways   117

10.   The Bradford Charter   132

11.   Titus Salt and S. C. Lister   142

12.   Education   152

13.   Modern Bradford   169

     Index   189

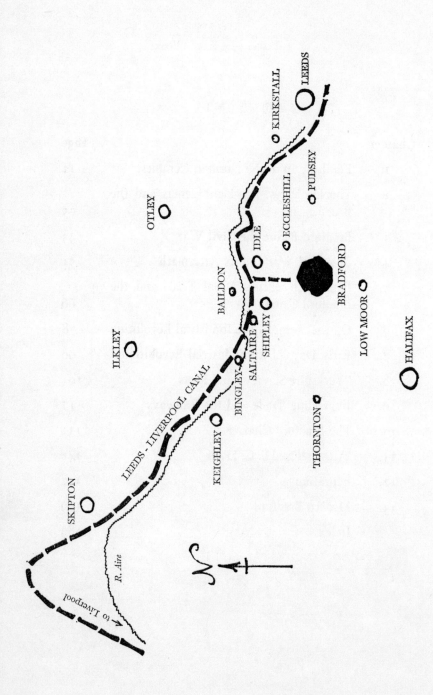

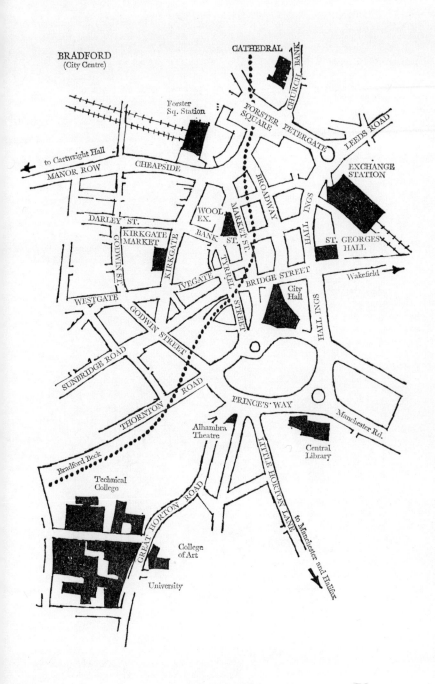

BRADFORD
(City Centre)

CATHEDRAL

CHURCH BANK

Forster
Sq. Station

FORSTER
SQUARE

PETERGATE

LEEDS ROAD

to Cartwright Hall

MANOR ROW

CHEAPSIDE

EXCHANGE
STATION

BROADWAY

HALL INGS

DARLEY ST.

WOOL
EX.

MARKET ST.

KIRKGATE
MARKET

BANK

ST. GEORGES
HALL

GODWIN ST.

KIRKGATE

ST.

TYRREL STREET

BRIDGE STREET

Wakefield

WESTGATE

IVEGATE

City
Hall

HALL INGS

GODWIN STREET

SUNBRIDGE ROAD

THORNTON

ROAD

PRINCE'S WAY

Manchester Rd.

Alhambra
Theatre

Bradford Beck

Central
Library

LITTLE HORTON LANE

to Manchester and Halifax

Technical
College

GREAT HORTON ROAD

College
of Art

University

KEIGHLEY
PUBLIC LIBRARIES

1. BRADFORD UP TO THE NORMAN CONQUEST

For signs of life in Bradford before the Norman Conquest we have to rely upon odd scraps of archeological evidence: the excavation of a burial mound, the discovery of a stone head, or the unearthing of a heap of Roman coins. All these help, but the conclusions to be drawn from most of the finds are very limited. It is like trying to assemble a jigsaw puzzle with many of the pieces missing: the final picture can only be completed by intelligent guess-work.

John James, who wrote about the town in 1841, took a very gloomy view of its past, saying:

> I prefer . . . that the history of this period, with regard to Bradford should be considered as nearly a void, rather than fill it with futile imaginations.

Since then many discoveries have been made, but we are still not very much nearer certainty than was James about Bradford's early history.

With the passage of time traces of older civilisations decay or disappear, but natural features change slowly. The beck which supplied Bradford's mills with water also slaked the thirst of Iron Age men, and footballers at Odsal play in a trough hollowed out during the last Ice Age.

Many old walls are built from stones left behind by a glacier which at one time filled Airedale. The glacier dammed up the streams which normally flowed into the Aire, with the result that lakes formed in all the side valleys, including Bradford-dale. As the volume of water increased the lakes overflowed one into another, carving out great channels in

11

the hills. The cavity at Chellow Dene and the huge bowl at Odsal were both caused by this kind of action. When the glacier receded it left the countryside strewn with rocks and boulders, many of which had been carried down from the Craven limestone district.

The first men to settle in Bradford would find themselves in possession of a natural basin on the lower eastern slopes of the Pennines, six to eight miles across, with one outlet northwards through the narrow gap into Airedale—a course taken by Bradford Beck. The beck, with such tributaries as remain, now flows under the city centre, but until the mid-nineteenth century it ran like any other stream, completely uncovered, making a large bend at what is now Bridge Street, before heading for the Aire three miles away. At present, when chimneys almost outnumber trees, it is difficult to realise that Bradford-dale must once have been a singularly beautiful and attractive spot—a small amphitheatre enclosed by wooded slopes and well supplied with gentle streams.

Earliest traces of human life, however, were found not in the sheltered dale but on the wind swept moors of Harden, Baildon and Ilkley, where round barrows were excavated more than a hundred years ago. The men and women of the Middle Bronze Age, whose dust and ashes were found in burial urns there, preferred the safety of exposed heights to the lurking dangers of thicketed slopes. The same terrain had also been well traversed by Stone Age hunters, who left behind their means of livelihood—an abundance of flint arrow-heads, scrapers, axes and other implements, but no human remains. The valleys, still occupied by glacial lakes, or at best treacherous swamps, were even less attractive to people who were beginning to settle down as farmers.

The moors to the north and west of Bradford, particularly those across the Aire Valley at Baildon and at Ilkley—Rombalds Moor—were once dotted with cairns, barrows and earthworks, and if excavation had been carried out in a systematic way we should now have an impressive record of prehistoric sites. Unfortunately, long before archeologists turned their attention to the neighbourhood, most of the sites had been disturbed and the stones taken for road making. In addition, the business of excavation was left to amateurs and enthusiasts who did not always value their finds. Many objects fell into private hands and disappeared without trace.

In the 1840s an Ilkley solicitor named Colls excavated a round barrow in the angle of an L-shaped double embankment on Baildon Moor. He discovered portions of two urns containing ashes and human bones, but both the urns and their contents have vanished. The mound has gone too, and only the embankment is left, together with a few of the stones which encircled the mound.

Chance finds also play an important part in the story. In 1880 a man working on the land at Lower Headley, near Thornton, uncovered three funeral urns; while in 1921 workmen making preparations for Chellow Heights Reservoir struck a burial mound where they dug out three urns which held human bones after cremation. Like others, these relics gave away few secrets. All we know is that the barrows, usually circled by stones, were constructed by people living between 1700 and 1000 BC, who cremated their dead, placing the calcined bones in earthenware urns, sometimes with a small food vessel alongside them.

The West Riding is millstone grit country, and if early men had purposely set out to baffle us they could hardly have set a more difficult problem than that of the cup-and-ring markings left on some of these large stone boulders and rock outcrops. The "cups" are small hollows two or three inches in diameter, while the "rings" take the form of shallow channels cut into the rock, so as to encircle the cups. No two patterns are exactly alike. Some are "cup boulders" only, while on others cups and rings make quite complicated designs.

Stones bearing these strange devices appear all over the world, but in Britain they are confined mainly to the north. The district around Rombalds Moor and Baildon, between the Aire and the Wharfe, seems to have been the centre of the activity, since more cup-and-ring stones have been found there than in any other place. Mere weight of numbers proves little, however: all we can say about the stones is that they date from the Early Bronze Age, 2000 to 1700 BC, and that the markings were probably of magical or religious significance. Many theories have been proposed, one that the craft developed from cave paintings, but certainty once again is lacking.

A more recent chance find occurred in 1965 when two schoolgirls walking through Heaton Woods picked up a strange stone which, when cleaned, proved to be a carved head with a base, complete in one piece. The features—small, thin mouth, pointed chin, wedge-shaped nose and prominent eyelids—suggested a head of Celtic origin, such as might have stood in a sacred grove or in a chieftain's house. It would have been an important discovery at any time, but the special significance of the find was that it sparked off an interest in local archeology, particularly of the Celtic period. Since then in Bradford and the surrounding districts stone heads of all kinds have come to light; more than in any other part of the British Isles.

The fine collection at Cartwright Hall covers a period from

the Early Iron Age onwards, but none of the heads can be accurately dated, and no one knows what purpose they served. Heads played a significant part in pagan Celtic religion, head hunting and the display of heads, both real and stone, being of great importance. Some of the heads have hollows in the crowns, which would enable them to be used as "fonts", while others have "cigarette holes" in their mouths, a special feature of Iron Age Celtic heads. Whether they were idols, household gods, or guardian spirits, is a matter for conjecture.

In addition to the considerable number of Celtic heads, the discovery of a succession of beehive querns, or hand mill-stones, of the same period, strengthens the belief that this district was once a well populated part of the territory ruled by the Brigantes, a group of Celtic tribes who resisted the Romans with immense ferocity. Yet while the main power of the Brigantes seems to have been concentrated on the lower slopes of the Yorkshire Pennines they made the whole of the north theirs as far as Scotland, from sea to sea.

The Brigantes probably encountered Ostorius Scapula and his forces near Chester in AD 51, after which their Queen,

Cartimandua, made a pact with him. But they were treacherous allies. Ten years later they helped the Iceni, under Queen Boudicca, to plunder Colchester and London, and most rebellions after that owed something to their turbulence.

In AD 71 a new Roman Governor, Petilius Cerialis, made war upon them in their own territory, engaging in fierce and bloody battles. In spite of this the Brigantes, supported by Caledonian tribes we know as the Picts and Scots, continued to defy the Roman Army until Agricola took command, and it was he who brought the north into subjection by a determined campaign ending in AD 79.

But the peace did not last. Agricola was called home and rebellion followed. Finally it was left to the Emperor Hadrian to build a wall which kept the Picts and Scots at bay for nearly three hundred years; and once the Brigantes were deprived of help from across the border they ceased to be a serious menace to the Roman forces.

In the north the Roman policy was to drive straight roads through the country, placing forts manned by regular troops at strategic points. Once a district had been subdued, however, the native chief was left in command, under military supervision. The kingdom of Elmet, for instance, which included Leeds, and some think Bradford, had its own native ruler even after the Anglo-Saxon invasions.

Roman roads branched out from York and Chester, the two main northern strongholds, and Bradford-dale lay in the centre of the Tadcaster-Manchester-Ilkley triangle, by-passed on all sides. The situation of the fort at Ilkley, *Olicana*, an important road junction, made it a place of some consequence, but Bradford did not appear on the Roman map.

Roman remains in this district are not spectacular, and although it is hard to believe that the armed forces did not visit Bradford at all during the four hundred years of occupation, there is little to suggest that they stayed. Roman coins have turned up in many places, the biggest collection being a hundred pounds' weight of silver denarii in 1776 at

Morton, where it was once possible to find traces of the Roman road from Manchester to Ilkley. This road, after skirting the boundaries of the present city at Denholme, went on to cross the Aire near Bingley, and it is thought that the brass chest containing the coins was buried en route by troops on a hurried march. A smaller hoard found on Idle Hill may have been left by soldiers who camped there for a time; but a solution which would account for most of the occasional finds —odd coins here and there—is that Britons in these parts had learnt to trade with Roman money.

Dr Richard Richardson, the eminent botanist who was born at Bierley Hall in 1663, concluded from the discovery of a number of copper Roman coins in a heap of cinders that iron had been mined there in Roman times, an opinion which received support when similar slag heaps in the neighbourhood were found to contain unsmelted iron. Whether the industry was carried on by the Romans themselves, or by native Britons who had learnt the craft, we are not sure.

Another speculation of more than usual interest concerns Tong Street. This street, about a mile long, is now modernized beyond recall, but its name stands out in isolation among all the roads, lanes and gates leading to Bradford. It was the continuation of a highway from Drighlington, which branched off the York-Chester Road. Because of this there is a theory that Bradford was built on a Roman road running from Castleford, via Tong Street, Ivegate and Westgate, to Elslack. But maps based on latest research show only an "uncertain" road from Drighlington, which ends where Tong Street reached Dudley Hill, about a mile and a half from Bradford. As Bierley is only a short distance from this point it is possible that iron from mines and forges there was transported along this route.

The older historians, at least, seem fairly certain that where a road had "the emphatic and isolated name of *Street*, a Roman road lay in the same direction." *Street* comes from Latin *via strata*, which means 'a paved high road' and the word *stret* was used in Bede's day to denote a Roman way.

B

This certainly seems to suggest that Tong Street had Roman origins.

No one knows who first preached the Christian gospel in this country, but somehow, while Britain was under Roman rule, the Church became so firmly established that by AD 304 it claimed its first martyr, St Alban.

Bradford has one small link with Christianity of the Roman occupation: Eccleshill. The first part of the name almost certainly goes back to the Celtic word *ecles*, from Latin *ecclesia*, meaning "church", showing that there was a place of worship at Eccleshill, perhaps before the Romans left. Apart from this, Bradford's slender legacy from the Roman era consists of a number of coins, the sites of iron workings, and a street which may have been a Roman road.

It is believed that the British tribes gradually moved down from the heights to make their homes in valleys, on the banks of a stream, or where two streams met; a choice which would guarantee both a supply of water and shelter from fierce winds. The site of Bradford fits this description perfectly, and it is highly probable that there was a Celtic settlement in this secluded spot. Those who chose Bradford-dale would be assured of a generous rainfall and a certain amount of good pasture in the clearings. Celtic farmers no doubt viewed their sheltered position with great satisfaction, but later inhabitants have often had cause to regret the choice of a site so near and yet so far from the main trade routes.

Long before the Romans were recalled in AD 407 to defend their homeland against the Goths, Germanic tribes began to make raids across the North Sea. The Britons were in an unenviable position, for while under the protection of Roman arms, they were liable to attack by Picts and Scots from the north, and by Angles and Saxons from the east. Finally, when left to their own resources, the Britons appealed to Rome for help, and were told to defend themselves as best they could.

When the full scale invasions from the Continent began in

AD 449 the southern Britons, through long dependence on Rome, had forgotten how to fend for themselves, and their territory was soon overrun. Beyond the Humber, however, resistance was stronger and the northern tribes, well prepared by years of skirmishing, came into their own. They were not completely subdued until after AD 600, when Elmet, the last British kingdom east of the Pennines submitted.

The English formed the kingdoms of Deira and Bernicia, roughly corresponding to Yorkshire and Northumberland. The two were later united as Northumbria, and Bradford would probably take its name as a Northumbrian township, a small group of hutments surrounding the dwelling of the headman or thane.

It is a far cry from a domestic scene such as this to the streets of fashionable Rome; but if Bede's story is true, the presence of a few fair-haired Yorkshire lads, on sale as slaves in the market place there, changed the whole course of history. Bede's account tells how a young deacon called Gregory was so touched by the sight of the angelic looking boys that he asked where they came from and who their king was. He was told that they came from Deira, a country ruled by King Aella. From that moment he determined to convert England, and when he became Pope sent Augustine to carry out the task.

Augustine with his band of missionaries landed in Kent in AD 597 and thirty years later Bishop Paulinus converted Edwin, King of Northumbria. At some time during his stay in the north Paulinus preached at Dewsbury, the mother church to which Bradford originally belonged, and a reminder of this ancient tie is still maintained by a payment of eight shillings made annually at Easter by the Provost of Bradford to the Vicar of Dewsbury.

Place-names are one of the great gifts of the Anglo-Saxon period, but they have one drawback: they do not carry dates. A few Celtic names have survived in the West Riding—*Leeds* (*Loidis*), *Ilkley* and *Chevin* among them, while *Aire* and *Wharfe* possibly belong to a pre-Celtic period. But most of our place-names and surnames were given to us by the German invaders, after one of whose tribes we were called *English*.

Wherever a name ends in -*ley* (*Bierley*, *Bingley*), it means that the settlement was made in a clearing in the woods. The commonest ending -*ton*, from -*tun* (*Bolton*, *Heaton*), was first used for any enclosed piece of ground or community of people, although later the meaning expanded to *town*. Other suffixes, -*ham* (*Manningham*), -*wic* or -*wick* (*Eldwick*), -*worth* (*Haworth*), denoted farms, villages or homesteads.

Bands of English invaders who strayed from the Roman roads on their way west towards the Aire Gap, would find their march across Bradford-dale impeded by a small but swift flowing stream between steep banks. The most convenient crossing place would be where a clearing had been made in the thick woodland near the foot of present day Church Bank—at the broad ford. This is what *Bradford* means, but some writers have expressed doubts as to how an otherwise smallish stream should suddenly become wide at a crossing place. The explanation given in *Place-names of the West Riding of Yorkshire* is:

> The ford was presumably one which carried a wide road across Bradford Beck in the centre of the present town.

This assumes that the approach road was broad, not the beck itself. But the ford was at the beck's lowest point of descent before leaving the town; that is, where Church Bank joined Kirkgate, in what is now Forster Square. The Parish Church used to be called *The Kirk i' the Wood*, and after a clearing had been made hereabouts, with the passage of many feet, too, the water would tend to form a shallow pool.

A suggestion that *Brad* comes from *brae*, 'a hill', giving the meaning 'the ford at the foot of the hill', is not borne out by the Domesday Book, where the name is written *Bradeford*. Another early spelling is *Brafford*, while old residents were known to refer to the town as *Brafforth*, or *Bradforth*. A simple way out of the difficulty is to accept the explanation that the beck is not nearly as wide as it used to be.

For nearly a hundred years, until AD 685, the kingdom of
Northumbria was supreme in affairs of Church and State, and
long after the death of Bede continued to promote both learn-
ing and the Christian faith. Wilfrid's church at Ripon dates
from AD 671 and the three ornamental crosses at Ilkley
indicate that a Saxon church existed there. It is probable that
Bradford's church dates from this period, but the only
tangible evidence consists of two pieces of a Saxon cross, one
built into the inner north wall, near the sacristy, and the
other at the entrance to St Aidan's Chapel.

The Danish raid on the monastery at Lindisfarne brought
the new English nation to its senses, its rulers having become
so accustomed to peace that they neglected to guard their
shores. No large scale invasion followed for a long time, but
in AD 866 the dreaded "great army" entered York, and
Northumbria ceased to exist. Yorkshire, in the south-east of
the kingdom, was divided into three parts, *thridings*, Bradford
being in the *West Thriding*— and it is not difficult to see why
this soon became West Riding.

Another invasion was made at this time by the
Norwegians, who, having rounded Scotland, occupied the
Western Isles and parts of Ireland. Although they ruled York
for a time, the main area of their settlements came to an end
just west of Bradford, where Norse endings like *-garth*, and
-thwaite, occur less frequently than in Lancashire and Cum-
berland.

Life would probably not change much under the Vikings,
and there is very little to remind us that they were ever in the
West Riding at all. Certain of their words remain, however,
and local speech still retains *laik*—"to play"; *skeller*—"to
warp"; *addle*—"to earn"; *natter*—"to worry", and, of course,
beck—"stream". *Hall Ings*, one of Bradford's central
thoroughfares, is so much part and parcel of the city, that the
name goes unquestioned in spite of its strangeness; but the
shops and offices there are built on land which once formed
meadows—the *ings*—owned by the tenant of the hall, later
the manor house. The ancient township of Leaventhorpe,

which had a fulling mill in medieval times, gives us the combination of what is believed to be an Anglo-Saxon personal name, *Leofwine*, with the Danish ending -*thorpe*—"farmstead".

We may well picture Bronze Age man busily at work on cup-and-ring stones at Baildon; red-haired Brigantians smelting iron at Bierley, and fair skinned Deirans farming on the uplands near the beck; but the first recorded fact about Bradford does not occur until 1086, when the Domesday Book was compiled. This "description" of the land was to tell King William "how it was held, and by what men". All the entries are in Latin, and the following is a translation of the account given of Bradford:

> Manor. In BRADEFORD with 6 berewicks, Gamel had 15 carucates of land to be taxed, where there may be 8 ploughs. Ilbert has it and it is waste. Value in King Edward's time £4. Wood pasture half a mile long and half a mile broad.

So, after moving among shadowy, nameless figures for hundreds of years we are at last in the company of flesh and blood. Gamel owned Bradford, and Sindi, Archil and Stainulf owned other manors in the district, just before the Conquest. Gamel, from his name a man of Viking descent, was lord of the largest estate, with six berewicks or outlying farmsteads dependent upon it.

Land measures varied a good deal from district to district and we are by no means sure what a *carucate* was. The word comes from Latin *carruca*, "a plough", and is usually explained as the amount of land a team of oxen could plough in a year, roughly a hundred acres. In Domesday *carucate* is used for arable land, and *hide*, a measure of about the same size, for pasture. An *oxgang*, a term we often meet in documents of this period, was the amount of land an ox could plough in a year, roughly an eighth of a carucate, or twelve acres.

On this reckoning Gamel had 1,500 acres of cultivable land

in patches here and there, among the woods and waste throughout the manor. Allowing ten acres to every family and five persons to each household, John James arrives at a total population of 750, with about 250 in Bradford itself.

Unlike Tong village, also described as a manor, Bradford was not "nucleated"—not compact. It consisted of the "chief vill" at the broad ford and six unnamed, scattered hamlets, with Haworth, almost certainly one of them, lying ten miles to the west. Yet Bowling, little more than a stone's throw from the ford, was a separate manor, as were Bierley and Wyke. Bolton, owned by Archil in King Edward's time, was only valued at ten shillings, but included land at Chellow, Allerton, Thornton, Clayton and Wibsey, worth forty shillings.

There is little agreement about Bradford's six berewicks, but Haworth, Manningham and the Hortons are first choices, with Oxenhope, Stanbury, Heaton, Idle and Denholme contending for the remaining places. Eccleshill had the distinction of being one of the king's own manors.

When the estates in Bradford dale were given to Ilbert, the new Norman lord, they were all described as "waste", a term unexplained by William's scribes. In 1069, three years after Hastings, the Conqueror had come north to suppress a rebellion which was being helped by Danish forces from overseas. His revenge was swift. Throughout the North and East Ridings a savage massacre took place, and the fact that so many manors were declared waste indicates that the "harrying of the north" extended to Bradford and the West Riding. If the phrase *vasta est* does not refer specifically to William's campaign of destruction, it might simply mean that the manors were in an impoverished state.

The details recorded in the Domesday Survey varied greatly from region to region. Information was given about mills, beehives, churches, vineyards, pigs, ferries and a host of other things on which a value could be set. But Bradford, in the Wapentake of Morley, received brief, routine treatment. One of the scribes, in a leisure moment, might have been able to add, however:

At the broad ford there is a chapel-of-ease among the trees on the hillside overlooking the vill; a hall where Gamel used to stay on his journeyings from manor to manor—since rebuilt in stone from nearby quarries and used by Ilbert de Lacy as a halting place on the way from his castle at Pontefract into Lancashire; not much iron in the manor itself, but supplies easily obtainable from Bierley and Wibsey; enough beehives to ensure small quantities of honey and wax, both expensive and in constant demand; sheep gradually returning to the hill farms as peasants move in—many of them "foreigners"—from outer districts; no shortage of pigs; no mill provided by the lord yet, but hand-grinding still meets the modest needs of the villagers; good fishing in the becks and River Aire. Bradford is not yet big enough to have a market, and it will be some time before the woods are cleared and the paths through the dale made safe enough for travellers carrying merchandise.

2. THE DE LACYS, THE PLANTAGENETS AND THE BOAR LEGEND

It was a strange stroke of fate that linked an unimportant village in the West Riding with a quaint little town in Normandy; but among those fighting side by side with William at Hastings were two brothers from Lassy. One of them, Ilbert—de Lacy, as he was known in this country— became lord of the manor of Bradford, a reward given to him, along with many other estates, for services to "our Duke William".

With an army of seven thousand William sought to subdue a nation of over a million people and for six years he was given little peace. Rebellion followed rebellion, and reprisals were swift. News that the Norman garrison at York had been seized and all the defenders put to death reached William as he was out hunting. He swore "by the splendour of God", his favourite oath, that those who had done these things would suffer. The harrying of the north was a barbaric massacre of men, women and children, many of whom scarcely knew an invasion had taken place. Fire and sword, succeeded by famine, carried off a hundred thousand between the Humber and the Tees. It took Yorkshire fifty years to recover from the destruction of life and the very means of living.

Bradford shared the common fate and according to the Domesday Book was left waste. Ilbert is thought to have led the attack on his future tenants, and for the thoroughness with which he did the job received a hundred and fifty manors in a fifty mile stretch of land between the Aire and Calder, Pontefract marking the east boundary and Clitheroe the west. The gift of another hundred estates in the Midlands and further south made him one of the most influential barons in the

25

country. What Ilbert gained, English thanes and freemen lost. Many who resisted were slain and the survivors were dispossessed of their lands. A few fortunate ones, like Gamel, had a portion of their property returned to them.

The "Frenchmen" were hated throughout the country and their lives were in constant danger. Fear of murder and sudden death led to the erection of castles on high mounds whereever a lord had his chief seat—work into which unwilling Englishmen were pressed. William encouraged castle building and it was at his suggestion that Ilbert de Lacy constructed the stronghold at Pontefract, a task which took twelve years to complete. In the meantime Ilbert is believed to have made his home in the old castle at Barwick-in-Elmet.

The King travelled the country from one castle to another, hunting where he pleased in the wide forests. The de Lacys and other nobles imitated the King's way of life as they toured their scattered estates, attending to business here and holding a court of justice there. Ilbert de Lacy visited his northern manors, passing from his headquarters at Pontefract, via Leeds, into Blackburnshire, and it is most likely that before tackling the inhospitable moors leading to the Pennines he would take rest and shelter at Bradford, a town lying directly along his route.

The approach of the lord's retinue was a thing to be feared by the local people, for they never knew what demands would be made upon them, or what kind of service they would have to perform for his comfort. If the lord felt especially well disposed towards his tenants he would order a bonfire to be lit for the general enjoyment of the whole village, and after the rejoicing Bradford would return to the grim business of getting a bare living from the soil.

The death of Ilbert de Lacy, early in the reign of William Rufus, is not likely to have been an occasion for great mourning among the peasant classes. To them, one de Lacy was as good, or as bad, as another.

Robert, heir to the estates, joined the baronial revolt which aimed at putting Robert of Normandy, the Conqueror's eldest son, on the English throne. He escaped "gallows and cord", the fate of some of the rebels, but was banished for life along with his son, a second Ilbert, who had also taken part in the rebellion. After this the course of events is not very clear. Reconciliation between the de Lacys and Henry I must somehow have been brought about, for we hear of Ilbert fighting courageously against the Scots at the Battle of the Standard, and later much of the de Lacy property returned to its owners. Ilbert, the third Baron of Pontefract, married Alice de Ghant, whose possessions passed to a more famous relative, John of Gaunt, future lord of the manor of Bradford.

The Normans were men of action who, when not too busy fighting to save the Holy Places, used their energy and their subjects' money to build huge monasteries and cathedrals with soaring spires. There is a strong tradition that Hugh de Lacy, Robert's younger brother, became Abbot of Selby, and that he was responsible for erecting the present Abbey church.

Henry, second son of Robert, found the pomps and vanities of the wicked world so attractive that once, when at death's door, he promised to build a monastery in honour of the Blessed Virgin if ever he should recover. His prayer was answered and true to his word he sent for the Abbot of Fountains, giving him land at Barnoldswick and sufficient money for the job. But the scheme was not blessed. A plague of rains lasting nearly a year destroyed their crops. At the same time a plague of robbers plundered the site and carried off their valuables; adversities which convinced Abbot Alexander that it was time to shake the mud of Mount St Mary from his feet.

His thoughts turned to a band of hermits he had encountered in his travels down the Aire Valley. They had settled in a quiet spot on the river-side near Leeds, an ideal place for an abbey. Having persuaded the hermits that their souls were in danger through their imperfect way of life, he went off to Henry de Lacy to obtain permission to move to Kirkstall, where he at once began to build a church and a Cistercian monastery.

The Cistercian monks, clothed in undyed wool spun and woven from the pure fleece of the sheep, came to the north of England from Citeaux in Burgundy at the request of Archbishop Thurston of York. Their first foundation in Yorkshire was at Rievaulx and the next was at Skelldale, near Ripon, the abbey from which Alexander was called to fulfil Henry de Lacy's promise.

The influence of Kirkstall Abbey extended to Bradford where, according to tradition, the monks owned Wibsey and much of the land around. Wibsey Fair, one of the oldest in the country, was said to have been granted to them by royal charter soon after the abbey was built. Burnett Field Estate was given to the Abbot of Kirkstall by the de Lacys. The first recorded tenant was Thomas Sharp, in 1459, the rent payable to the Abbot of Kirkstall being "½d half yearly at Pentecost and St Martin's-in-the-winter, 14 November, and a pair of white silver spurs". Law Beck divided the estate into Upper and Lower Burnett Field, the former being in Bowling, the latter in Horton. In later years a windmill stood by the beck and the little row of isolated cottages in Smiddles Lane are still known as the *Mill Houses*.

Although Bradford was a town of rising importance in the twelfth century it could afford no permanent resting place for the bones of Norman barons and their families. Henry de Lacy was buried in the abbey he had built, and the funeral cortege of his son Robert probably passed through Bradford on its way to Kirkstall from Clitheroe Castle. The presence of Robert at Richard I's coronation indicates that the family was now fully restored to royal favour, and their fortunes prospered accordingly.

John de Lacy took part in the Third Crusade and died fighting at Tyre in 1190. His son, who had accompanied him, was more fortunate. Roger, the most notorious of all the de Lacys to date, returned, a fierce and brutal campaigner, to assume his father's titles. The Welsh, by no means gentle fighters themselves, nicknamed him "Roger Hell", because of his vigorous attacks upon them. Not content with war at home, he went to Normandy to command Chateau Gaillard for King John, but fortune deserted him and he was captured.

A high price was set on Roger's head and the King himself subscribed a thousand marks towards the required sum. As tenants were often bound to find a part of any ransom demanded for their lord, we may wonder how much the people of Bradford had to scrape together to get back one who, despite his reputation, had done them very little good.

Roger was foremost among the great northern barons of his day, and his son John, Earl of Lincoln, Baron of Pontefract and Blackburnshire and Constable of Chester, came only a little way behind in prestige. He opposed King John and was one of the twenty-five barons appointed to enforce the conditions of Magna Carta. After being excommunicated by the Pope he submitted to the King and was pardoned. Crusading was still very much the fashion, and John, no doubt to ease his conscience, went to the Holy Land in 1218. He returned safely and was buried at Stanlaw in 1240.

By this time Bradford had attained a fair degree of prosperity, paying 5 marks in *tallage* to the King when Leeds only paid 3½ marks. But if we read that Bradford ranked as one of the chief towns in Yorkshire we must remember that it was nothing like the size of York, which had a population of five thousand or more.

One thing which placed a town "on the map" was the grant of a market, a jealously guarded privilege obtained by royal charter. In 1251, a year which was a landmark in the history of Bradford, Henry III gave "our beloved valet Edmund de Lacy" permission to hold a market in the town every Thursday. In fact, the traditional market day was Sunday, when the families in the dale, from all the scattered villages round about, attended Mass at the Parish Church. It was very convenient to combine business with pleasure and religious duties, and it is not surprising that in spite of protests from the clergy, Sunday markets continued to be very popular. They must have been the highlight of many a dull, tedious week. The parish extended for fourteen miles, the only other church being at Haworth, and it was not to be expected that people would make what was often a long and hazardous journey twice a week.

In Bradford, as in many other places, the market was held in the churchyard. In very thriving towns the lord would build a permanent market place with surrounding plots for tradesmen's houses, but the de Lacys did not consider Bradford worthy of such expense. Edward I passed a law making it illegal to use churchyards as market places, but the custom persisted at least until the reign of Elizabeth when, in an effort to keep the minds of the faithful on heavenly things, traders were forbidden to show their wares until after morning service.

When Edmund de Lacy died, his widow, Alice, received Bradford as part of her dower, in return for which she paid the King something like £4,000, a huge sum which is said to have gone towards the cost of building Westminster Abbey. The owners of benefices—churches and church lands—were very jealous of their rights as patrons, and we owe the first mention of the church at Bradford to the fact that, in 1281, Alice endowed it with ninety-six acres of land and presented the rectory to Robert Tonnington.

Much of our detailed knowledge of day to day life in medieval England comes from surveys of estates which were usually made when they changed hands. From an *Inquisition* of 1277 we learn that:

Henry de Lacy hath many liberties in the town of Bradeford; to wit, a gallows, assize of bread and beer, a marketplace and a free court from ancient times.

The medieval system provided instant justice, with a gallows at hand in case of need. In Bradford the place of execution is thought to have been at Bowling, near to the old iron works, where there was formerly a field called Gallow Close. Complaints and charges were dealt with by the lord or his officials "on the spot" and in the reign of Henry VII the inhabitants protested because the Court Baron, which used to be held every three weeks had been discontinued.

Preserving law and order was a profitable business and the "free" court was a good source of income. Fines for assault were particularly heavy: ten shillings where blood was drawn and 3s 4d for an assault without bloodshed—in comparison with which "6d spent on gallows" represents a very modest outlay. The assize of bread and beer entitled the lord to keep watch on the weights, measures and quantities of these two important items of medieval diet. Those who infringed the law could expect little mercy: fines were heavy and punishment severe.

The *Inquisition* contains the following unusual entry:

And they say that Nicholas de Burton, steward of Henry de Lacy, had Evam, weaver, of Gumersal in the prison at Bradeford, and took from him two cows, and him permitted to go without judgment.

This shows that weaving was being done near Bradford at a very early date. Whatever crime poor "Evam" had committed —he was probably in debt—cost him two cows and a spell of imprisonment.

In 1294 Henry de Lacy obtained a charter for holding markets and fairs in various towns belonging to him, Bradford being one of them. Here he was given permission to hold a five day fair on 31 July, the eve of the Feast of Blessed Peter in Chains, but later the date was changed to St Andrew's-tide, 30 November. Why November, with its short, dark days, should be preferred to July is difficult to understand, but getting the harvest in may have had something to do with the change, or perhaps a clash with neighbouring fairs.

In the same year there was a dispute between the Earl of Lincoln and the Lord of Horton which shows how much boundaries have changed. Henry claimed three acres of land

from the wastes of Horton in the Turles (Tyrrel Street) "for
the attachment of his mill dam and for ease and liberty about
his mill of Bradford". Hugh de Horton contested this claim
and, as a result, obtained a deed by which Henry de Lacy and
his heirs were required to pay three shillings annually for the
land, which must surely have been bounded by the Bradford
Beck and the water running to join it from Cuckoo Bridge—
Bowling Beck. Thus, the City Hall stands on ground which
was once in the township of Horton.

The *Inquisition* of 1311, made at Pontefract shortly after
the death of Henry de Lacy, has been described as the most
correct and important document concerning this part of the
country, after the Domesday Survey. It takes account of all
the Earl's possessions and gives invaluable information about
Bradford in the Middle Ages. Like all the documents of the
period it was written in Latin: it goes into great detail and
only a few extracts can be given here.

> The Earl had at Bradford, a Hall or manor house,
> with chambers, and it is nothing worth beyond
> necessary repairs. . . .

And there is one Water Mill, valued by the year, at	£10	0	0
And a Fulling Mill, which is worth yearly	£1	0	0
And there is a certain market, every seventh day, upon the Lord's Day, the toll of which is worth yearly	£3	0	0
And there is there a certain fair, which is held annually upon the Feast of Saint Andrew the Apostle, the toll of which is worth yearly	£3	0	0

Many of the items deal with land holdings, one being:

> The Abbot of Kirkstall, for four oxgangs of land in
> Horton, a pair of white spurs.

This was no doubt the Burnett Field Estate already mentioned. "Spur tenure" was quite common among the *Petit
Serjeanties*, as this type of contract was called, and "a pair of
white spurs", which James gives as *par' calcar' al'*, may have
been made of silver or of whitened metal. One spur was not

unusual, "One spur (*calcariam*) of Lincoln", being the rental
for property in Elkesley, Nottingham. But because *calcaria*
also meant *lime*, or *lime kiln*, Blount, in *Ancient Tenures*,
says, "However, to dissemble nothing, and not to conclude
too rashly, it is possible that *calcaria* may signify a load of
lime."

Another entry concerns twenty-eight burgage houses, the
nucleus of the town, which lay along Kirkgate, Westgate and
Ivegate. These were the houses of the burgesses, who, as
skilled craftsmen, were a cut above labourers and tillers of the
soil. As the Poll Tax returns of 1379 give the names of three
innkeepers it seems likely that the Bradford of Henry de Lacy
would boast a similar number of inns somewhere along the
"three starved streets".

The hall, because it had chambers, was the kind of manor
house we usually think of, with private apartments for the
lord and his family at one end. Why it was barely worth
maintaining goes unexplained, but one possibility is that the
Earl was so busy about the King's business that he had little
time to look after his own affairs. Some writers believe the hall
was built with stones taken from an earlier castle, which had
either been demolished or fallen into ruins, but no actual
record of a castle exists and no site has been found.

The water mill, mentioned for the first time here, was a
great asset to a community, but an even greater asset to the
lord, for all his tenants were bound, under pain of stiff
penalties, to grind their corn at the mill and pay "soke". This
"rake-off", a portion of everything ground there, was bitterly resented by the people, but the importance of the toll
can be gathered from the fact that the annual value of the
Bradford mill amounted to a quarter of the entire income
from the manor. The presence of a fulling mill confirms the
belief that cloth making was well established by 1311. The
market was now held officially on the Lord's Day and the fair
had been transferred to November.

The makeshift Saxon church had been replaced a hundred
years earlier by a sturdy stone building with thatched roof,

c

which looked down on the hall and the little settlement enclosed by the beck—the craftsmen's houses with their crofts and tofts; a few shops and two or three inns; the villeins' one-roomed cots scattered here and there; the well worn path ending at the water mill; the ings where the lord's beasts grazed, and some way further off the two or three communal fields.

Working on the basis of 130 families John James estimated that the population of the town would then be 650 persons.

Great houses rise and fall, and with the death of Henry, Earl of Lincoln, in 1310, the long reign of the de Lacys, lords of Bradford for nearly 250 years, came to a glorious end. Henry, who was only a boy when his father died, was brought up at court, as a result of which he became the favourite and confidential friend of Edward I.

His distinctions read like a roll call of honour. Always in the forefront of battle, he was chief commander of Edward's army in Gascony during the invasion of France in 1297, and two years later led the vanguard against the Scots at Falkirk. When the court was held at Carlisle he was given precedence over all the peers except the King's sons. He was Custos of Knaresborough Castle and began to build the castle at Denbigh, where a statue in his honour was placed over the gate.

Henry died in London, at Lincoln's Inn, which was named after him, and was buried in St Paul's Cathedral.

Although Henry de Lacy enjoyed fortune and public fame his private life was a tragedy. Of his four children, two sons were killed and one daughter, Margaret, died before him. Having no male heirs he put the family estates at the disposal of his old friend Edward I, who regranted them to Henry for life, with the provision that they should then pass to Thomas, Earl of Lancaster, husband of Alice, Henry's surviving daughter. For reasons which are not very clear, Bradford, once again, was separated from the other de Lacy possessions, and left to Henry's widow, Joan. It then passed by right of marriage to her second husband Nicholas, Lord Audley, who became the new lord of the manor.

The Earl of Lancaster through his wife, assumed all the privileges of the de Lacys, and would have owned Bradford eventually if he had not plotted to overthrow his cousin, Edward II. The quarrel with the King's favourite, Piers Gaveston, was maintained, it is said, at the death-bed request of Henry de Lacy, and was complicated in no small way by the conduct of Alice, Thomas's wife. According to the old historians Countess Alice was a "lewd woman", who was aided and abetted by the King in a love affair with Earl Warren. Things came to a head in 1317 when the Countess was carried off one day from her home at Canford, in Dorsetshire, by a deformed knight, and taken to the Earl of Warren's castle at Ryegate, a plot in which the King had part.

Thomas was the recognized leader of the barons who were in rebellion against the King, and became the most powerful nobleman of his day, especially after Edward's downfall at Bannockburn. He was defeated, however, at Boroughbridge in 1321, and suffered the ignominy of being executed outside his own castle at Pontefract.

Thomas was a most popular hero and after his death, people, possibly with another Thomas in mind, made pilgrimages to his tomb. His claim to sanctity was due, no doubt, to his reputed generosity to the Church and to religious foundations, but he has gone down in history as a "Sunday saint and Monday devil"—cruel, stupid, brutal, jealous and immoral: as John James puts it, "deficient in firmness of soul and perseverance of conduct".

In addition to confiscating all Thomas's lands the King compelled Joan, Henry de Lacy's widow, to hand over the manor of Bradford, upon which it became a crown possession, a distinction which did it little good. In 1327, when Edward III became King, Parliament granted the Lancaster estates to Henry Plantaganet, Thomas's brother, but Bradford was held for some years by Queen Philippa.

The next owner was Henry, Earl of Derby, who held the manor of Bradford when an *Extent* was taken in 1342. From him it descended to his daughter Blanch, who married John of Gaunt, fourth son of Edward III, but towards the end of his life John of Gaunt gave Bradford to his son, John de Beaufort, Marquis of Dorset. In 1399, when John of Gaunt died, Henry Bolingbroke, the next heir, was in exile, and before he could claim the estates Richard II siezed all his uncle's possessions, including Bradford; but in the same year Henry overthrew the King to become Henry IV.

From this time onwards Bradford Manor had a chequered history. It was often leased to the highest bidder, and the tolls from markets and fairs, as well as the rights of the corn mill, were farmed out for profit.

James I settled the Honour of Pontefract on his Queen; but to clear his father's debts Charles I sold the manor of Bradford, along with most of the other estates, to the City of London in 1628.

The first half of the fourteenth century was a time of great distress in the north. Edward II's defeat at Bannockburn in 1314 was the signal for a series of devastating raids by the Scots on the West Riding, which had given special help to the King's armies. Bradford, where the church was almost completely destroyed, appears to have suffered so badly that rents and land values declined everywhere. By 1342 the annual value of the water mill had gone down from £10 to £6 6s 8d, and that of the fulling mill to a mere eight shillings.

After Bannockburn came the Black Death, which is said to have reduced the population of the country by nearly a half. Bradford was badly affected by the plague, and thirty years later, from the Poll Tax return of 1379, we get the following details.

Bradford	26 married couples, 13 single men and 20 women;
Manningham	7 married couples, 2 single men and 3 women;
Horton	17 married couples, 2 single men and 5 women;

while of Bolton it says, "No one remains in the township, therefore nothing collected". Even allowing for a considerable amount of tax evasion the return indicates a large decline from John James's estimate of 130 families in Bradford in 1311.

The Poll Tax, which was bitterly resented by all, was levied by Richard II to help to finance his wars. All people over sixteen had to pay according to their station, beginning with 4d for those of no particular trade—a man and his wife, or a single person. In Bradford three innkeepers topped the list at 12d, followed by two tailors, two shoemakers, one fuller and one mason, all at 6d.

In all, Bradford paid 23 shillings; more than Halifax (12s 8d), but a very small amount when compared with Pontefract (£14 10s), Doncaster (£11 13s 4d) and Wakefield (£4 15 8d).

An interesting name on the Bradford list is "Thomas Walker, Fuller". Fulling mills were often called "walk mills" because in the finishing process men used to tread the fuller's earth into the cloth in order to remove the grease and impurities. Later, instead of "walking", the cloth was beaten with heavy wooden hammers, and they were turned by a mill. In 1342 the Walker brothers were tenants of both the fulling mill and the corn mill, and their names appear in Bradford records for many years after this.

Tentering, the process of stretching the cloth on frames after fulling, was a frequent source of fraud, a favourite trick being to stretch the cloth and then thicken it, where it was weak, by applying paint mixed with wool waste. King's officers, called "ulnagers" were employed to measure the length and width of the cloth, test its quality and fix their seals on it, but in spite of this there was still much dishonesty. The name of William Walker appears in the ulnager's accounts of 1472, a year when Bradford received its first mention.

In 1597 a vain attempt was made to stop "the deceitful stretching and tentering of northern cloths", by forbidding tentering altogether, on pain of death. But without tentering there could be no finished cloth, and the ridiculous Act was not enforced.

The Walkers, perhaps because of their unpopular trade, were often the victims of assault. One attack upon them is recorded in 1358, when William de Bradeford and Matilda his wife were charged with having pursued Thomas Walker to the "Shamels", up Westgate, where they wounded him with a knife, called a "twitel". The Walkers' house was later beseiged and blood drawn. Another of these business differences occurred when Lord Adam Boulore, chaplain, on a journey to the dyehouse at Bradford, where he was taking his cloth to be dyed, fulled and tentered, was met by John le Webster on the bridge. The chaplain stabbed John on the shoulder, whereupon John took revenge, wounding the other with his twitel and laming him.

Just as the *Inquisition* of 1311 gives us a general picture of medieval Bradford, so in the *Extent* of 1342 we have a thumbnail sketch of the life of a villein or bond tenant called John Reins, who rented a cottage and an oxgang of land, paying 3s 3½d yearly, including 3½d for release from harvest work. The *Extent* continues:

He also renders 12d yearly at the term of St Andrew by a custom called Thistletake, for which payment all the swine of his own rearing shall feed in the wood of the lord in the time of pannage. . . . And, with the bondmen he shall make and repair the mill pond whenever it is required. And he shall fetch grindstones for the said mill . . . and also the timber required for the repair of the mill within the lordship, receiving every other old grindstone, and a moiety [i.e. a half] of the old timber for his reward. For labour in repairs of the milldam he shall have a measure of meal per day in common with his fellow bondmen in Bradford and Manningham. He shall also be reeve or granger of the mill, and also woodward when the vacancy occurs, but have no remuneration from the lord for this service. And he shall, with the bondmen, carry the victuals of the lord, with a horse and man, from Bradford to Haworth and Colne, and thence to Ightinghill, receiving at every township 4d. And he shall carry with them wood for the lord's use on his journey, and also wood for the enclosures on the manor, and what may be required at the mill, and receive for every ten horse loads, 1d. And he shall not marry his daughters, nor permit his sons to marry, without permission or license of the lord. . . . And when he shall die, the lord shall receive nothing, save that the holding shall remain in the hands of the lord until the wife or next-of-kin shall satisfy the entry.

Poor John Reins! We are not told what use he had for old grindstones, or how he found time to till his own ground. Yet the picture is not as black as it seems, for this man became one of the largest landowners in the manor and the tenant of the corn mill, ending his days as a person of considerable means.

So far we have been tracing the history of Bradford through archeological remains, charters, tax-lists and battles. Now we come to a strange episode, half fact, half legend—a story which has outlived the manor house and the corn mill and given the city its coat of arms. The legend, as told by James Hartley, a schoolmaster who lived in Bradford during the eighteenth century, runs as follows:

A ravenous wild boar, of most enormous size, haunted a certain place called the Cliffe Wood, and at times very much infested the town and the neighbouring inhabitants thereof; so that a reward was offered by the Government to any person or persons who should bring the head of this boar; which much excited some to attempt it.

Now the story runs thus: that this boar frequented a certain well in the aforesaid wood to drink, which to this day is called the Boar's Well; that he was watched by a certain person who shot him dead there, took his tongue out of his head, and immediately repaired to court to claim the promised reward.

Presently after this departure from the well, another person came thither upon the same intention, and, finding the beast dead, without any further examination, cuts off his head, and away he hastes towards the same place and in expectation of the same reward as the former, and there arrives before him; being introduced into his Majesty's presence, the head was examined, but was found without a tongue, concerning which the man being interrogated could give no satisfactory account.

Whilst this was held in suspense, the other man was introduced with the tongue, claimed the promised reward, and unfolded the riddle by informing his Majesty how and

by what means he had killed the beast; and thus received the following grant, namely, a certain piece or portion of land lying at Great Horton known by the name of Hunt Yard, and for the tenure of which he, and his heirs for ever, should annually attend in the market-place at Bradford, on St Martin's Day in the forenoon and there, by the name of the heir of Rushforth, hold a dog of the hunting kind, whilst three blasts were blown on a Gelder's horn and these words,

> Come heir of Rushforth, [or Rushworth]
> Come hold me my dog,
> Whilst I blow three blasts of my horn
> To pay my Martinmas rent withal.

The historical part of this story has its origins in the fact that before money came into wide and general use land was often granted in return for services and gifts which, like "a pair of white spurs" or "two white hares", make little sense to modern readers. Even stranger is the payment made yearly to one, Godfrey Bosville, of "a snowball at midsummer and a red rose at Christmas", for a farm at Langsett in the parish of Penistone.

In 1342 a certain John de Northrop had been granted three cottages and six oxgangs of land in Manningham in return for:

> presenting himself every year at the Feast of St Martin at the Manor of Bradford, prepared to go with his lord as far as Blackburnshire, for the space of 40 days, with one lance and one dog, to take the wild boar, receiving from the lord daily for himself 1d and for the dog ½d.

Besides assisting in the boar hunt, John had to be prepared to go with the bailiff to Pontefract as often as required "as safe conduct for the lord's money", and this at his own expense. He was also ordered to attend at court every three weeks and, as usual, had to surrender his best beast when he died. The only cash payment due from him was 8d to be released from work on the lord's land at the spring sowing. Another tenant, Roger de Manningham held land rather confusingly at Horton, on similar terms.

When John of Gaunt was lord of Bradford he toured his estates in shining silver armour at the head of a grand procession of retainers on richly caparisoned horses. These visits must have been great events for the ordinary people, and to make them even more imposing John Northrop was ordered to sound a horn as his lord approached. For this service, and the cost of the horn, his Easter payment was cancelled.

A descendant of the Northrop family afterwards granted land to a man called Rushworth of Horton on condition that he helped with the horn-blowing ceremony, holding the dog, while Northrop's man sounded the call, the formula being as before "Come heir of Rushworth. . . ."

"Horn tenure" is quite ancient, as may be seen from the gift of the Rangership of Bernwode Forest, in Buckinghamshire, made by Edward the Confessor:

> with a hide of land, to Nigell and his heirs to be held by a horn. This Nigel had killed a large Boar there, and this was his remuneration.

As in the Bradford story the wood was "infested by a boar", which was slain by Nigel the huntsman, who presented the boar's head to the King. The Bradford version refers to "his Majesty", which is usually taken to mean the lord of the manor, but in view of the above example the wording may be a relic of an early document. To complicate matters further, however, it must be said that there is no written tradition of a tongueless boar in Bradford before about 1780.

Hunt Yard can still be seen at Great Horton, while a plaque on a house at the top of Kensington Street reminds us that Girlington formed part of the Hornblow Lands, which the Northrops owned for almost five hundred years. A horn used at the above ceremony went with the Hunt Yard property and passed through many famous hands, including those of Richard Fawcett and Sir Titus Salt. The "Bradford Horn", now in Bolling Hall, is of uncertain date, but we know that the silver mounting was added in the nineteenth century.

As a result of this mixture of history and tradition, when the town was granted a Charter of Incorporation in 1847 it was given a coat of arms bearing the head of a tongueless boar, a well and "three Bugle horns stringed Or", the whole topped by a sprig from Cliffe Wood—"the Trunk of a Tree sprouting proper".

3. BRADFORD BEFORE THE CIVIL WAR

The great national event of the fifteenth century was the struggle between the houses of York and Lancaster—the Wars of the Roses. Incredible though it may appear to present day "Yorkshire Tykes", the fighting men of Bradford, led by the Bollings, Tristram and Robert, took the side of the Red Rose, but as the manor was part of the Duchy of Lancaster their choice was not as strange as it seems. In addition, the powerful Cliffords of Skipton, bitter opponents of the Yorkists, put such pressure on the Bollings and other neighbouring lords that their lives would have been in danger if they had refused their support.

The Lancastrians were defeated at the battle of Towton in 1461, after which Edward IV became King and the Bolling estates were confiscated. Later, however, Robert Bolling pleaded for the return of his property on the grounds that he had only taken up arms because of the threats from John Clifford, and as he returned to live at Bolling Hall his request must have been granted.

Robert Bolling died in 1487 and the estates passed to his eldest son, Tristram. Tristram's daughter married Richard Tempest of Bracewell in 1497, receiving Bolling Hall and the estates as her dowry. In this way the manor of Bolling passed into the hands of the Tempest family.

While the nobles were settling their differences, the people of Bradford were slowly rebuilding the Parish Church, with private chapels for the Bolling and Leventhorpe families. The work was largely undertaken by the Vicar, William Rodes, but the piecemeal construction dragged on for over a century. The tower was not completed until 1508, quite fifty years after the main body of the church.

43

There were other churches near Bradford, at Calverley and Tong, for instance, but until 1606, when Wibsey Chapel was opened—now Holy Trinity Church, Low Moor—the only other place of worship actually in the parish was at Haworth. A record of 1466, however, refers to a wayside chapel built at the end of Ivebridge for the benefit of travellers. This chapel, with the strange dedication to St Sitha, is thought to have been similar to the one which can still be seen on the bridge at Wakefield.

The dedication has been the subject of much argument in the past, for there are two St Sithas, one the daughter of a Mercian prince, the other an Italian serving girl, Zita, or Citha. The English maiden, who became the patron saint of laundresses, met her death at the hands of Danish invaders; the Italian saint, renowned for her zeal in church attendance and her care for the poor, was invoked to find lost keys. The vanished chapel makes a strange little interlude in the story of Bradford, and the memory of St Sitha, whichever young lady is intended, is kept alive by a canon's stall in the Cathedral.

St Sitha is mentioned again by John Leland, Henry VIII's Antiquary, who dedicated the account of his travels to the King. Leland's *Itinerary* contains a famous description of Bradford, then a busy market town about half as big as Wakefield.

> BRADEFORD a praty quik Market Toune, *dimidio, aut eo amplius, minus* Wackefelda. It hath one Paroche Chirche, a Chapel of *S. Sitha.* It standith much by clothing, and is distant vi Miles from Halifax and 4 from Christestal Abbey.

At first sight it seems that Leland was a poor judge of distance, because Halifax and Kirkstall (*Christestal*) are certainly further from Bradford than this; but before the introduction of the statute mile standards of measurement varied a good deal from place to place. One explanation put forward is that Leland was using "customary miles", a measure about one-

and-a-half times the normal mile. According to the *Itinerary*, Leeds, at that time, was as large as Bradford, "but not so quik".

Bradford, then, stood "much by clothing", but in the fourteenth century it was as renowned for its boots and shoes as for its wool. Tanning was often mentioned in the Manor Court Rolls. In 1347, for instance, John, son of Thomas, faced a charge of witholding toll in respect of tanned leather, and in the same year Robert Goldsmith was fined twopence for carrying bark beyond the lord's moor without licence. In 1357 a Bradford tanner was charged at the court with polluting the beck with the sweepings of his tan house.

In Bradford the tradition of shoemaking was so strong that in an Elizabethan play called *George a Green, the Pinner* of *Wakefield*, King Edward IV is made to say:

> I think we are now in Bradford,
> Where all the merry shoemakers dwell.

A little later the Shoemaker addresses the King and his party, who are disguised, saying:

> Down with your staves, my friends,
> Down with them.

When the King asks why, the Shoemaker replies:

> My friend, I see thou art a stranger here,
> Else wouldst thou not have questioned of the thing.
> This is the town of merry Bradford,
> And here hath been a custom kept of old,
> That none may bear his staff upon his neck,
> But trail it all along throughout the town,
> Unless they mean to have a bout with me.

Another poet also mentions the "jolly shoemaker" of Bradford, who would not allow anyone to walk through the town carrying staffs upon their shoulders, for if they did "he soon should beat them down". He was a man of such strength and prowess that a rivalry sprang up between him and Robin Hood, whose grave, it must be remembered, is said to be at Kirklees Priory, Brighouse, only five or six miles from Bradford.

Barkerend Road probably owes its name to "bark houses" in the district, "barkers" being the men who stripped the trees and prepared the bark for the tan pits. There were once tan pits near Kirk Bridge, an area which appears to have become a dumping ground, because in 1684 the overseers of the highway at Bradford were ordered "to remove and carry away all the ashes that lie between the Church Bridge and the Tanhouse", and people were warned not to deposit any refuse there.

The Aire Valley has a long association with tanning, Leeds being an important centre of the industry in the 1880s, and at Cottingley the tan pits were not demolished until 1920.

So much credit has been given to Edward III for encouraging cloth manufacture in this country that it is sometimes thought no weaving was carried on here before the Middle Ages. There is no shortage of proof, however, that cloth was made in the West Riding long before history was written.

In Skipton Museum there is a fragment of a shroud recovered from the tree trunk coffin in which a Bronze Age man was buried about 3,500 years ago, and the Cartwright Hall collection contains spindle whorls found on Iron Age sites at Baildon and Shipley. In the days of hand spinning these whorls, usually made of stone or wood, were fitted on to the end of the spindle to keep it steady as it revolved. The large number of whorls of burnt clay left behind on Roman sites in Yorkshire suggests that spinning was, in those days, a common domestic occupation. All told, there is enough evidence to prove the existence of a continuous tradition of cloth making in this part of the country from the earliest times.

Gervase, a thirteenth-century writer, said that the art of

weaving seemed to be a peculiar gift bestowed upon the inhabitants of this country by nature, an opinion prompted no doubt by the number of flourishing weavers' gilds. The formation of the gild system established the various branches of cloth making as trades, and York became the great weaving centre of the north, quite overshadowing small places like Leeds, Halifax and Bradford.

For centuries after the Conquest, England was the only country from which foreign merchants could obtain sufficient supplies of wool. As a result it became the most important article of export, three-quarters of the entire customs revenue in 1421 coming from wool alone. The Woolsack in the House of Lords served to remind the peers that wool was the seat and foundation of the nation's economy.

English wars were financed by wool, and when Richard I was taken prisoner on his return from the Crusades, one year's supply of wool was borrowed from the Cistercian monasteries towards his ransom. Wool was so valuable that in the fourteenth century 2½ stones would buy an ox.

Edward III placed an export duty of £2 on every sack of wool and, in order to protect weavers at home, export of wool was forbidden altogether for many years. The regulations were easily evaded, however, and smuggling was rife. Sometimes imports of foreign cloth were banned or restricted and only wealthy people were allowed to wear garments made from it. The importance of the wool trade may be judged from the number of laws which hedged it about—so many and so intricate, that a Commission in 1622 said it was very hard to know what the law really was.

In view of the demand for wool, it is not surprising that sheep farming developed on a large scale. The hill slopes of the Pennines and Yorkshire Dales provided ideal grazing grounds and Kirkstall was one of the eight Cistercian Abbeys which between them controlled some of the finest sheep pasture in the world. Fountains Abbey, which kept huge flocks in the Kilnsey area, is said to have sold twenty-two tons of wool annually abroad, and Bolton Priory five, the chief buyers being from Northern Italy and the Netherlands. In 1292 Kirkstall sold all its wool for the next ten years ahead.

The wool was sent to the abbeys from outlying granges by pack horse, and green roads and trails can still be seen in some parts of the Pennines. Further reminders of this thriving trade are the narrow hump-backed bridges, like the one at Beckfoot, Bingley, with low parapets built specially to allow free passage to the pack horse trains. The proximity of Kirkstall must have been a factor in Bradford's development, because weavers were within easy reach of good supplies of wool and, of course, the abbot had an estate in Horton.

When Edward III came to the throne in 1327 he faced a crisis. Wool was as valuable as ever, but the manufacture of woollen goods had declined so much that the trade was no longer counted as a national asset. In Bradford, some measure of the general decline may be seen in the value of the fulling mill, which in 1342 was entirely unroofed and worth only eight shillings a year, in spite of the Walkers' monopoly of fulling throughout the Duchy of Lancaster.

Thomas Fuller, the seventeenth century Church historian, who had much to say about the wool trade, spoke in his usual quaint fashion of our weavers as being ignorant of their art, "knowing no more what to do with their wool than the sheep that wear it . . . their best clothes then being no better than friezes, such their coarseness for want of skill in the making." The material shrank badly, too, becoming "a giant to the eye and a dwarf to the use", so that the saying "to shrink as northern cloths" became a by-word. Frizinghall, neighbour to Saltaire, is thought to have taken its name from the frieze or frize cloths made there.

Flemish merchants took our wool and returned it with considerable profit to themselves as high quality cloth, but few countries wanted to buy coarse English woollens. Exports accordingly dwindled, and in towns like York and Lincoln, once famous for their cloth, only a handful of weavers were left. So, in an effort to encourage his own people to make better material, and thus revive a falling trade, the King decided to entice weavers from abroad by granting them protection and special privileges.

In 1331 Edward III sent letters of protection to John Kemp of Flanders, a woollen cloth weaver, to come over here with servants and apprentices, to exercise his trade and "to teach such people as were inclined to learn it". A large number of families, including weavers, dyers and fullers, accepted the invitation and settled in various places, encouraged, no doubt, by laws promising fair play and tax concessions. The Kemps set up business in York and were joined five years later by two weavers, Willielmus and Hankienus, both from Brabant.

Norfolk attracted a good share of these foreign craftsmen, but according to the Poll Tax list of 1379 there were only seven Flemish weavers in the whole of Yorkshire, and certainly none in Bradford.

In country districts, away from the large towns, the inhabitants were usually small farmers who turned to cloth-making as a useful side-line, especially on wet days. In Bradford, because there was so little arable land, the order was reversed and the people came to rely more on their looms and spindles than on their husbandry.

1631 was a year of abundant harvests, but the poor complained bitterly about the high price of corn, and King Charles ordered an enquiry into the stocks held by rich men. Bradford was one of the places where a thorough investigation was made and the searchers, having drawn a blank, reported that the country was mountainous and barren,

and the inhabitants thereof living mostly by trading, have not more corn than is sufficient for sowing the little ground they have.

A much later Agricultural Survey, in 1799, ends cryptically with the remark:

No practices can be pointed out here that would be of advantage in other districts; the inhabitants having both their minds and capitals fixed on trade.

D

As many writers have pointed out, it was Bradford's natural *dis*advantages from an agricultural point of view, that turned it into an industrial town, and fixed the minds of its inhabitants on trade.

4. THE CIVIL WAR AND ITS AFTERMATH

The bonds of the "old faith" were not especially strong in Bradford, and the changes brought about by the Reformation appear to have been received quietly. A hundred years later, when the Civil War broke out, the town was a Parliamentary stronghold. The manor was often in the hands of the Crown and when Charles I sold it to the citizens of London to pay off his father's debts the inhabitants of Bradford were hurt and displeased. They distrusted the King and hated Archbishop Laud, who had called one of the parish clerks before the Court of High Commission because he had conducted informal services.

Fears were abroad that "Popery was likely to be set up and the light of the gospel put out". Young Joseph Lister witnessed the weeping, fasting and praying that went on in many a household, "not any of us, old or young, eating so much as a morsel of bread for twenty-four hours together. . . . Mothers and children expecting daily when they should be dashed to pieces, one against the other." A highly coloured report, no doubt, but these were the fears that sent some off to New England and led others to take up arms against the King.

Lister's *Genuine Account* of the "sore calamities that befel Bradford in the time of the Civil War", is so "genuine" that its authenticity has been questioned. The *Account* keeps well to the main story, however, and is almost as much a part of Bradford's history as the events themselves.

One Sabbath Day in the autumn of 1642 Joseph Lister, then an apprentice lad of fifteen, having first obtained permission from John Sharp, his master, left Horton Hall for

51

Pudsey. This was a long walk he often took to hear Elkana Wales, a minister whose eloquence and fervour were such that he had been known to spend as long as six hours in the pulpit, preaching and praying without break.

On this occasion the service had not been in progress long, when the peace of the little chapel was shattered by a stampede of feet outside. The door burst open and the congregation turned, horrified and shocked, to see a man in a state of great distress. "Friends", he cried, "we are all as good as dead men; the Irish rebels have reached Rochdale. They'll be in Bradford before long." John Sugden, the bearer of the news, said no more. He turned and went as quickly as he had come.

Pandemonium broke out: women wept, children shrieked. Some, unable to restrain themselves, ran into the street shouting; and over the babel the voice of Elkana Wales pleaded for calm, and sure trust in God. Order was restored at last and the service, in spite of the interruption, went its full length.

Joseph Lister lost no time in getting back to Bradford, where he found little groups talking excitedly here and there. He learnt that a party of horsemen had been sent to Halifax to get the latest reports of the Irish rebels, and waited with the rest for the return of the messengers. The news they brought back disproved the rumours. What they had found was, not a horde of blood-thirsty assassins, but a few harmless Protestant refugees, who had left Ireland to escape persecution.

But if troubles were averted from one quarter, they came from another. The people of Bradford had voiced their opposition to the King and refused to obey the commands of Archbishop Laud. The result was a body of the King's foot and horse billeted in the town, awaiting orders to destroy it by fire and sword.

The townsfolk kept to their houses and prayed for deliverance. Once again their fears were groundless. For no apparent reason the troops were recalled, leaving the inhabitants to take fresh stock of the situation.

Neighbouring villages were consulted as to how best they might defend themselves in the event of another invasion.

Accordingly, barricades were set up at every entry to the town and spies kept watch on the enemy, who had camped at Leeds. Preparations to defend the town were speeded up and every able-bodied man and boy stood to with a weapon of some kind. But Bradford's "home guard" was ill equipped even by seventeenth century standards, for it faced shot and shell with nothing but farmyard implements.

Soon word came that the Royalists, or "Malignants", as the Roundheads called them, were on the move, and within a short time three companies had mustered at Undercliffe, less than a mile from the town. Joseph Lister gives an eye-witness account of the scene:

> ... the next morning they struck their tents and advanced towards us, and came to the brow of the hill, where they exhibited to our view their ensigns of war, which were truly very awful and tremendous to behold; here they halted and made every preparation to attack us. They were about seven or eight hundred men, we were about three hundred; they had several pieces of cannon; we had none.

The first burst of firing seemed to bring death and destruction from the skies, but in the hand-to-hand fighting the gallant three hundred defended the passes so well that the enemy could not break through.

Just as both sides were preparing for a long and bitter struggle something akin to a miracle happened. Snow began to fall heavily and a wind of hurricane force lashed the attackers on the hill, so that they were barely able to stand. Nor was this all. One of the great guns blew up, causing such fear and confusion that the entire army fled. The defenders, because of the storm and "other inconveniences", returned to the town to regroup their forces.

The Parliamentary army in the north had been placed under the control of Ferdinando Lord Fairfax, of Denton Park, Otley, a staunch Puritan whose son, Sir Thomas Fairfax, also held high command.

In his diary Thomas says, "The first action we had was at Bradford." But if "Black Tom" as he was known, visited the town in the early stages of the campaign it was only to collect troops to fight elsewhere, for he regarded Bradford as "very untenable". Indeed, firm faith was needed to champion Bradford's cause, for its fighting men were an untrained, leaderless rabble, "lacking both the head, body and sinews of war".

Help came, however, from an unexpected quarter. A certain Captain John Hodgson of Coley, near Halifax, hearing of Bradford's plight, was so moved that he offered his services at once. News that the Earl of Newcastle was on his way with strong reinforcements filled the Roundheads, as they were now called, with grim determination. "Conquer or die" became the motto.

The Captain mustered his men to find that about eighty had long guns or muskets. The rest were a motley crew armed with clubs, sticks, flails, scythes and sickles fastened to long poles.

His plan was to turn the church into a fortress: if that could be held the town might be saved. Ten or twelve of the best shots were placed in the steeple, and the rest in and around the church. Those with improvised weapons he stationed wherever an entrance seemed likely to be made. Then, using all resources, Lister tells us:

we . . . hung large sheets of wool upon that side of the steeple facing the road by which they were to approach us, so close to each other, and so nigh the roof of the church, that it would be with difficulty for a ball to penetrate the steeple.

(A "sheet of wool" is a sack—a woolsack—not a tightly compressed bale)

Several days of unexpected quiet followed, during which spies were sent out with orders to raise the alarm as soon as the enemy showed signs of movement.

Accordingly, on the 18th of December, being the Sabbath-day, the Earl of Newcastle sent the van of his army again from Leeds, consisting of five troops of horse, six troops of dragoons, and two hundred foot, commanded by Colonel Goring, Colonel Evans, Sir Wm. Savile and Sir John Gotheric, intending with these troops to surprise the town while the inhabitants were engaged in divine service; but our scouts returned and alarmed the town and country of their approach; and now what hurry and confusion immediately ensue; the whole congregation betake themselves to flight, and seek for refuge where they think most safe; every man is now ordered to his post, armed with such weapons as he was beforehand provided withal; the church and steeple secured in the best manner we possibly could, being determined (relying on Divine assistance) to defend it to the last extremity.

Again they approach us with the sound of warlike music and their streamers flying in the air. Tremendous sight! Enough to make the stoutest heart tremble, to shake the nerves and loose the joints of every beholder. . . . They then advanced nearer and set down in Barker End, not above three hundred paces above the church, where they raised a battery against it, but chiefly against the steeple, intending if possible to erase it to the ground.

And so the scene was set for the first siege of Bradford, the "Battle of the Steeple".

Seventeen times the great guns boomed out, but one man in the steeple picked off a cannoneer with his fowling-piece, a deed which so encouraged the rest that they swarmed up the bank in a surprise attack. The Cavaliers, although taken aback, kept their eyes on the target and moved their guns nearer the church, at the same time occupying a few houses and a barn lower down the slope. From this place they sent out Sir John Gotheric with a troop of horse to surround the town, but fire from a sentry near Westgate and the sudden arrival of a body of clubmen from Bingley soon caused them to return.

The cannon had now been directed towards Kirkgate, the

Woolsacks on church—Civil War

road by which reinforcements came to relieve the defenders. Cannon balls "whistled through the streets" but either because of bad marksmanship or good providence no casualties were reported.

Meanwhile the Bradford gunmen harassed the cannoneers, and those in the houses, by firing volleys whenever a buff or scarlet coat showed itself. But the large church windows exposed them too much and, tiring of the cat-and-mouse game, they decided to break cover. While the cannons were being loaded they left their posts and, backed by those in the streets, rushed furiously upon the houses. Those who resisted were killed outright: those who yielded were taken prisoner. The common soldiers among the Royalists did not distinguish themselves, but their commanders, conspicuous in red coats, bore the brunt of the scything and clubbing. Among all this, the church and the town still came under heavy fire.

In the heat of battle an unfortunate incident occured. A brave young officer, thought to be the Earl of Newport's son, led a company of footmen in a rash attempt to force a way into the church. He fell into an ambush and, being cut off from his men, begged quarter. On hearing this, one, Ralph Atkinson replied, "I'll give you Bradford quarter", and killed him. Later it was learnt that Atkinson had taken gold from the officer's pockets, as well as rings and other valuables, a rash action he afterwards very much regretted.

The footmen were so shocked by the death of their leader that they fled instantly, pursued by the Bradfordians, who killed several. By now the Royalists had packed their bags in preparation for retreat, which they did, Lister says, "using their feet better than their hands". Not content with victory, fifty of the defenders followed them for a mile and a half to Bradford Moor, shooting and clubbing for dear life. Then, after a long day's fighting, the pursuers returned footsore and weary, pausing no doubt at the top of Church Bank to admire, in the evening gloom, the church tower scarred but intact against the skyline.

On the Bradford side casualties were few; only two or three

killed and a dozen wounded, but the King's army had suffered badly, losing three officers and any number of men. There was great rejoicing in the home camp, not least because of the amount of booty taken, which left them better off than before the siege. The victory, against such tremendous odds, was seen as the Lord's doing, for a handful of unskilled men had routed a thousand well armed troops trained for war.

The following day a trumpeter came to demand the body of the Earl's son, which was given to him.

The Christmas of 1642—no special time of rejoicing for Puritans—passed without incident. In January 1643, a month after the siege, Sir Thomas Fairfax, the "Rider of the White Horse", came to Bradford at the head of a small company to let the town see that its heroic deeds had not gone unnoticed. Having recruited a few more men he decided to attack the Royalist garrison at Leeds, where, with banners flying and the war cry "Emmanuel" on their lips, the Roundheads performed valiant deeds. In less than two hours the day was won, the spoils being a good store of arms and five hundred prisoners.

Upon hearing of this disaster the Earl of Newcastle's forces at Wakefield and Pontefract fled to York, returning when the coast was clear. From Leeds, Fairfax marched to Selby, and then quickly turned about to attack Wakefield, once again in enemy hands. During this encounter Fairfax narrowly escaped capture, but his men were able to mop up the town, taking fourteen hundred prisoners, in an action described as a miracle rather than a victory. The Earl of Newcastle, undeterred by defeat, called up ample reserves and prepared to tackle his opponents on their own ground at Bradford.

After more than a year's continuous fighting the Roundheads were feeling the strain. They had insufficient men for a sustained campaign and provisions were low—down to twelve days' supply. From this point Lord Fairfax himself directed operations; grouped his forces, a mere three thousand men, and made a plan to intercept the Royalists at Whisket Hill (Westgate Hill), three or four miles from the town.

The Roundhead march was timed for the early hour of four on the morning of 30 June 1643, but Major General Gifford, who was responsible for marshalling the troops, delayed the move until after seven, thereby laying himself open to suspicion of treachery. By that time the Royalists were drawn up in full battle array on Adwalton Moor, ready and waiting. Lord Fairfax sent his men straight into the attack, one forlorn hope meeting another on the slope of the hill. The defenders were driven back and the Roundheads gained a footing on the edge of the moor, where counter-attacks according to Sir Thomas, received a "hot welcome".

So far, in spite of their superiority in numbers, especially in cavalry and the inevitable cannon, the "Malignants" were getting the worst of things. Indeed, some of their men, thinking the order to retreat had been given, left the field. But at this crucial moment, when the battle hung in the balance, a charge of Royalist pikemen upon the Roundheads' left turned the tables.

It was the wavering Major Gifford who, Sir Thomas says, "did not his part as he ought to do". The account does not enlarge upon the defeat: the Parliamentarian forces were routed, and the whole army retreated to Bradford. As the direct way to Bradford was barred they made their return by a roundabout route, Sir Thomas towards Halifax and his father in the direction of Leeds.

The Earl of Newcastle lost no time in marching to Bolling Hall, the home of Richard Tempest, which he made his headquarters for a second attack on Bradford. Joseph Lister takes up the sad tale:

> . . . our troubles begin again; fresh storms arise, and clouds of sorrow gather blackness over our heads, threatening us with greater distresses, if possible, than heretofore; for the Earl of Newcastle . . . immediately marched a most formidable army towards us, where he sets down at a place called Bowling-Hall, and presently comes forward to a place convenient for his purpose, where he directly points his

cannon upon the town, but more especially against the church and steeple, as if he was determined to revenge himself of that place from whence he had of late met with such severe treatment.

Out came the woolsacks again and the town prepared for a second siege. This time, however, the mood was different: there was no talk of "Conquer or die". Soon the cannoneers, showing off their marksmanship, hit the cords holding the woolsacks and—sad omen—brought them down, amid loud cheers.

The position now seemed hopeless and the Earl of Newcastle's offer to negotiate was gladly accepted. During the truce the Royalists moved their cannon to Goodman's End (Bridge Street) and completely surrounded the town. When the talks broke down late in the evening it was the signal for a furious barrage from the newly placed battery, which brought the following lament from Lister:

Oh! that dreadful and never-to-be-forgotten night, which was mostly spent in firing those dreadful engines upon us, so that the blaze issuing therefrom appeared like lightening from heaven.

At dead of night, Thomas Fairfax, who had been left in command by his father, called a council of war. With only one barrel of gunpowder left, and not a single match in the town, it was decided to abandon Bradford in order to get as many of the army as possible away to Leeds, now in Parliamentarian hands.

The next day Fairfax led a charge of twelve horsemen against three hundred Cavaliers, and succeeded in getting through with two of them. The rest, including Lady Fairfax, who was riding behind one of the officers, were captured. A similar disaster befell the foot soldiers, of whom only about eighty broke through the cordon. The others returned to the town and surrendered. A touch of real gallantry was provided by the Earl of Newcastle, who dispatched Lady Fairfax to her husband in his own coach, with guards to ensure safe conduct.

Joseph Lister pauses in his narrative, to ask his readers to put themselves in the shoes of the unfortunate inhabitants of Bradford.

Every countenance overspread with sorrow, every house overwhelmed with grief; husbands lamenting over their families; women wringing their hands in despair; children shrieking, crying and clinging to their parents; death in all his dreadful forms and frightful aspects, stalking in every street and corner.

Yet, though the town was plundered, the people were spared. The story goes that the night before the dread order of execution was due to be given, the Earl of Newcastle, lying comfortably in a four-poster bed at Bolling Hall, was disturbed by an apparition. One version implies that there was a kind of tug-of-war for the bed clothes, which the ghost tried to remove. "Pity poor Bradford; Pity poor Bradford", the creature wailed; and whether this caused the Earl to repent, or whether his intentions were not so dastardly after all, the fact is that only those who had offered resistance were killed.

The troops ransacked the town, pillaging all that was valuable and doing wanton damage. What they could not carry away they threw into the streets. Chests and sacks of meal, feathers and chaff from mattresses—all were strewn about everywhere. Livestock was rounded up and driven to Bolling Hall where it was offered for public sale.

It was this sight that greeted Joseph Lister as he made his way back from Colne, where he had been to see his master, Mr Sharp, a staunch Puritan, who was doing duty in Lancashire. His task was to find Mrs Sharp and take word back to her husband.

Having found Mrs Sharp safe and sound, Lister returned to inform his master, telling him, however, that their only cow had been taken by the Royalists to the open market. His mission now was "to buy our own cow, or another, get our grass mown, and stay together".

His adventures with the cow read like a pantomime story.

No sooner had he bought the cow than the soldiers came by night and took it back, a process which was repeated until the boy grew tired and let them keep it.

Although the actual fighting in Bradford lasted for only a few hours, the effect of the Civil War upon the town was very serious.

In 1642 burials at the Parish Church numbered 145, and in 1643, when the battle of Adwalton Moor was fought, the total rose to 493, but many of these deaths may have been due to the plague. In 1644 there were 149 burials, and in the following year the number fell to a more normal 74.

Lord Clarendon referred to Leeds, Halifax and Bradford as "three very populous and rich towns, which depending wholly upon clothiers naturally maligned the gentry". These clothiers were sturdy, outspoken nonconformists, who, as events showed, would not submit silently to interference in either their religion or their businesses.

Just before the war began, it is estimated that about ten thousand people in Bradford and the nearby Aire Valley towns were employed in making coarse, narrow cloths called kersies. In 1626 a charter was granted to Leeds in recognition of the revenue it had brought to the Crown by skilfully exercising "the art or mystery of making and working woollen cloths commonly called in England "Northern Dozens". . . to their perpetual praise."

But traders could not expect much from Puritans who didn't believe in fairs or holidays and who wore the plainest of plain clothes. Bradford received few favours from Cromwell's Government, and its status sank so low that, unlike Leeds and Halifax, it was not allowed the privilege of sending a member to Parliament. In 1659 "The Trade of Cloathing" —and Cromwell—"being dead", Sir Thomas Fairfax and others petitioned for a free Parliament, in the hopes of better business.

The harsh laws against dissenters, which came into force soon after the accession of Charles II, were keenly felt in

Bradford, and in 1663, a year after the Act of Uniformity was passed, a number of townspeople joined in a plot to overthrow the new régime. The conspirators met on 12 October in a wood at Farnley, near Otley, to put their plans into operation; but they were faint hearted, and the arrival of a troop of horse sent them packing. Many of those who were implicated went abroad, but twenty-one poor unfortunates, none of them from Bradford, were put to death at York in January of the following year.

At about the time of the Farnley Wood Plot the Vicar of Bradford, Jonas Waterhouse, who may have been one of the conspirators, refused to comply with the Act of Uniformity and, after some wrangling, retired from the living. He was replaced by the Rev Francis Corker, a man who was no stranger to Bradford. Mr Corker's exploits have made him a legendary figure, and if the stories about him are true he was a remarkable man though not a very admirable one.

Francis Corker was Vicar of Bradford when the Civil War broke out, the living having been presented to him by Charles I. He was a Royalist who, when his position in Bradford became untenable, left to join the King's forces, becoming a chaplain to the garrison at Pontefract. During the siege of the castle, when all seemed lost, he led a party of men through the enemy's lines and obtained relief from Oxford. After that he served as spy and guide to the King, performing deeds of daring while two horses were killed under him. Eventually he was taken prisoner, but escaped from Lincoln Gaol the night before he was due to be executed.

After the King's defeat he changed sides and at the Restoration was imprisoned in the Tower as a traitor. His services to Charles I stood him in good stead, however, and after a pitiful appeal he was released and allowed to return to Bradford, a "sadder and a wiser man". We are not told what kind of a welcome awaited him, but he remained Vicar until his death in 1667.

Two years before this, Bradford received a severe setback from an outbreak of plague, the infection being conveyed from London, it was thought, in a bundle of old clothes. Those who contracted the disease were taken to Cliffe Barn, near Undercliffe, where they were left to minister to one another. Food placed on a stone at some distance from the barn was fetched by the more able and given to those who were too ill to walk or crawl. Stones found in a wood close by marked the graves where the dying buried the dead.

5. EIGHTEENTH-CENTURY WOOL TRADE AND THE BRADFORD CANAL

Towards the end of the seventeenth century Bradford was reduced to poverty, not by pestilence and famine but by a change of fashion—the vogue for cane-bottomed chairs. It had become largely a town of one trade, the manufacture of Turkey cloth, a fabric used for covering chairs and furniture, and the sudden lack of demand caused a crisis. In despair a petition was sent to Parliament, saying:

> Turkey Work is the staple Trade of the Town of Bradford, whereby the Poor have had their Livelihood; But since Cane Chairs have been in use, the Trade hath decayed, and is lost, which formerly consumed Eight Hundred Packs of Wool; And now the said Poor, that used to be so employed, beg their Bread, and the Town, and others near it, without some Redress, will come to Ruin, and Praying that the House will take their Case into Consideration.

The Petition was referred to a committee, but Turkey work did not return to favour, and no special measures were taken to help the town.

In view of the poor state of trade, the Court Rolls of 1678 contain a puzzling order, designed to restrict cloth manufacture in the town, or so it seems. It warned:

> That the inhabitants of Bradford shall not let any houses to persons to be clothiers, upon pain of 39s 11d every month; nor set to work any fit to be servants except datal men.

Perhaps it was an attempt to protect the established clothiers by keeping out newcomers, a suggestion which gains support from a much earlier order imposing exactly the same fine on anyone entertaining strangers "without the consent of the constable and four freeholders". Whatever the case, the order did nothing to revive the trade in woollen cloth, which gradually died out in Bradford.

Daniel Defoe made a tour of the north in 1720. He had a good deal to say about Leeds and Halifax, but nothing much about Bradford, except that it had a market and was the birthplace of Archbishop Sharp. Leeds had a cloth market which Defoe thought unequalled anywhere, while the industry of the Halifax people amazed him. There, every house had its own rill or gutter of running water, and a tenter frame on which a piece of cloth was stretched. All were busy:

> some at the Dye vat, some at the Loom, others dressing the Cloths; the Women and Children carding or spinning, all employed from the Youngest to the oldest, scarce anything above Four years old but its Hands were sufficient for its own support.

Although Defoe appears to have let his enthusiasm run away with him, Halifax, at this time, was one of the leading woollen towns in the West Riding. Bradford had not yet attained prosperity, and the number of poor in the parish had increased to such an extent that in 1738 it was thought necessary to build a workhouse. But families were in being like the Hustlers, Garnetts, Rands and Fawcetts, who were to set the town on the first stage to becoming "Worstedopolis", the wool capital of the world.

Nothing annoys a true Bradfordian quite so much as to hear the city described by some innocent stranger as "a woollen town", for while it is true that Bradford's fame rests fairly and squarely on wool, most of the output from its mills is "worsted", pronounced "woosted" by those born and bred in the trade. The Flemish weavers who brought their special craft to England in the fourteenth century settled, as we have seen, in Norfolk, but it was the little village of Worstead (Woosted), not the county town, Norwich, which gave its name to the fine, smooth cloth known throughout the world for its excellent qualities.

Almost any book about Bradford will sooner or later go into the difference between *woollen* and *worsted,* some in great technical detail, but here a simple description will do. The cloths are made by two different processes, with two different ends in view. Worsted yarn is made from wool which is *combed* to separate the short-fibred "noils" from the long-fibred "tops". In the combing process the long fibres, straight and parallel, are made into a smooth rope or sliver called a top. The drawing-out process continues and the fibres are twisted to give a strong, supple yarn. The finished cloth, not fulled of course, shows a clear, clean, well defined pattern.

Woollen yarns are *carded* (*card* coming from Latin *carduus,* "a teazle") and the pins on the carding rollers "tease" out the wool and criss-cross it, so that the yarn, when woven, gives a felted appearance to the cloth, the best example being flannel. Fulling completes the matting process. *Cloth,* properly speaking, refers to woollen material or material generally: *stuff,* is the real name for worsted.

In fairly recent times, wool for worsted yarns has been carded, too, as a preparation for combing, the fibres being laid roughly parallel to one another: but woollen yarns are not combed.

Long before machinery came into general use, Bradford and the West Riding had begun to take over the worsted industry from Norwich; and although the word *industry* must call to mind smoking mill chimneys, the truth is that before the year 1800 factories were almost unknown, and cloth making was still a cottage industry. It was usually a case of, "Betty spinning: self weaving".

The diary kept by Cornelius Ashworth of Waltroyd, near Halifax, gives us a glimpse into the daily life of a clothier in 1782. On 14 October he carried a piece to his employer and got paid for it. On the same day he wove 4½yd and the next day 9yd. For a week he was busy with the harvest and weaving took second place. On 23 October he resumed work at the loom, added two more yards and then mended his coat. Next day he churned till ten and wove 6½yd. The 25th was wet, so he spent all day at his loom, weaving 8½yd. On one occasion he took a day off, and by way of recreation went to see two men hanged on Beacon Hill.

In this part of the country one of the first signs of the Industrial Revolution was the rise of "manufacturers", who were men with enough capital to buy wool in bulk; have it processed; pay out wages to combers, spinners, weavers; and wait for their profit until the finished pieces were sold.

A man like John Hustler, woolstapler-manufacturer of Bradford, had to be prepared to spend much of his life in the saddle. We can imagine him setting off on horseback in the early hours of a spring morning, bound for Lincolnshire to buy a year's supply of long wool. Having struck his bargain, the long trek back to Bradford would be made in company with the packhorse train carrying its precious burden. Sorting and scouring would probably be done by "the master", with

Wool transported by pack horse

the help of his family, and the wool would then be handed over to combers, working in nearby houses at their "pots of four". Next came the business of distributing the tops to spinners in dozens of cottages up and down the dale, perhaps as far away as Keighley or Skipton. The spread of handloom weaving made it difficult to find enough spinners locally, four

being needed to keep one loom going. The wool was sometimes taken out of the district altogether, journeys of a
hundred miles or more not being uncommon, and the spun
yarn then had to be delivered to weavers nearer home. John
Hustler would probably take his pieces to the White Lion Inn,
Kirkgate, where a large sale room was reserved for the purpose on market days, but some manufacturers had a room on
their own premises.

The Hustler family were leading members of the Quaker
sect, whose meeting place was at Goodman's End, or Good-
manend, now Bridge Street. John chose for his wife Christina,
one of the ministers of the "Friends", and although he found
neither the time nor the inclination to marry until he was 48,
raised six children in comfortable circumstances at Undercliffe
House, which became both home and workshop. His income
might well have amounted to £1,000 a year, for "making
brass" was a second religion, and even God-fearing men saw
no need to pay very high wages.

The century in which John Hustler lived acts as a bridge
between rural Bradford, with a great central rookery near
Kirkgate, and a fine row of trees in Hall Ings—between this
secluded spot and the town soon to be made hideous by a
rising tide of mill chimneys. It was a period crammed with
event and action.

John Hustler was born a year too late for the accession of
George I, but in 1715, when he first saw the light of day, the
bells of the Parish Church rang out to celebrate the defeat of
the Jacobite rebels at Preston. It was fear of a return of
Catholicism which led families like the Hustlers to raise sums
of money to support the Hanovers, and ensure a succession of
Protestant rulers. The Quaker community was not very
numerous but, like the German merchants of the nineteenth
century, its members were a powerful influence in the town.

There was panic during 1745 when rumour spread that
Bonnie Prince Charlie, moving south with his army, was
approaching the West Riding. Many inhabitants, like the
Hustlers perhaps, hid their valuables and prepared for the

worst; but confidence was restored by a regiment of Royal
Scots which passed through Bradford on its way to intercept
the rebel forces. Once more the church bells sounded a thanks-
giving peal.

The beginning of John Hustler's life was marked by war at
home and the end by revolt against English rule abroad—the
American War of Independence. Just before he died the
French Revolution broke out and four years later England was
at war with France again.

In time of war, invasion from across the Channel has always
been a possibility and "Home Guards" have often been
ordered to stand by for action, as in 1794 when Bradford
pinned its faith on the *Ready and Steady*, a band of volunteers
smartly attired in scarlet coats turned up with buff, white
breeches, black caps and bobtails.

The recurring threat of invasion stimulated a strong hatred
of French people and French ways, but Tom Paine's book *The
Rights of Man* appealed to revolutionaries in some places.
Bradford declared its loyalty by holding a procession in which
Paine's effigy, dressed as a stay maker, was carried through
the streets and burned along with copies of his books.

Volunteer bodies were formed on three occasions, nearly a
thousand men being called up in 1803, and the fact that Bradford ranged itself among the *principal* towns in compliance
with the Volunteer Act of 1782 must be regarded as a sign of
its growing importance. It may be that these forces were kept
in being as much to discourage unrest at home as to keep out
the enemy, for the north was specially suspect. Even after
1814 some levies were still under orders there.

Meanwhile the Mann brothers of Bradford gained world-
wide renown as manufacturers of artificial limbs, and in 1794
Admiral Pasley came to the town to have the loss of a leg made
good. After Waterloo, Lord Uxbridge and a Russian commander named Colonel Kutusoff found themselves in Bradford
on a similar errand, both awaiting one of Mr Mann's legs.

The fact that no fighting took place in Britain left men to
get on with their weaving and women with their spinning. It

also gave some men the opportunity to busy themselves with inventions which were to make fortunes, not for the inventors, but for those who used the new machines and perfected them.

In spite of wars, or perhaps because of them, national progress went on apace. In Bradford this prosperity was reflected in the decision to build a Piece Hall, "a very elegant and commodious hall". According to James Hartley the building was erected especially for the sale of worsted stuffs, such as calimancoes, which had become the chief staple trade of the town and neighbourhood.

John Hustler was the driving force: subscriptions came from all quarters and the Piece Hall opened in 1773. It stood in Kirkgate, a plain barn-like structure with a belfry and a flight of steps on each side, leading up to a stone balcony, which formed the main entrance.

> . . . this commanding position was found very useful for outdoor speakers at election and other times, there being plenty of space for a large audience in the neighbouring field. . . . Every Thursday morning at ten o'clock the bell was rung to summon all buyers of pieces, and at 11.30 it was rung again as a notice that the market was closed. At two o'clock the bell rang again, to show that the market was open; and at 3.30 p.m. it gave the signal for closing.

The Piece Hall provided a market for merchants from the surrounding districts and an extension was added to the premises. Trade eventually overflowed into the Old Market Hall on the site of the present Wool Exchange. John Hustler proposed to build a Market Hall with shops behind the Piece Hall, but William Rawson, lord of the manor, who owned the market rights, objected and the building was converted into a warehouse. Hustlergate, the short street nearby, dates from about this time.

The great need of any rising industrial town was a cheap and convenient means of transport. Before 1760 canals were unknown in England, but the "infernal roads", with ruts sometimes four feet deep, were all too familiar. Business men

Kirkgate market

were driven by sheer necessity to find an alternative to broken carts and over-loaded pack-horses, and turnpike roads were a partial answer to the problem. Although these new highways, with their toll booths, were much resented by ordinary people, they greatly helped the movement of goods and passengers. Two turnpike roads passed through Bradford, one from Selby and Leeds to Halifax, and the other from Wakefield to Kendal, via Keighley. A third went from Bradford to Ripon.

But the cost of transporting goods by water was only a fraction of the cost by road. In John Hustler's day ten packs of Irish yarn could be sent from Cork to Bristol for £1 10s, while the cost of getting the same load across country from Bristol to Norwich was £10.

The River Aire was navigable as far as Leeds, thanks to the Aire and Calder Navigation Company, but no similar enterprise had benefited Bradford. It was John Hustler, however, who set in motion the negotiations which led to the construction of the Leeds-Liverpool Canal; and the completion of the Bradford Canal, to form a link with it, owes almost everything to his foresight and perseverance.

Today the word *canal* conjures up a picture of stagnation, of preservation societies and week-end pleasure boats. The skill of Brindley, who designed the Bridgewater Canal; the toil and sweat of the navvies; the excitement at the opening of each new section of canal; the fireworks and general jubilation, have all been forgotten. But to James Hartley and his contemporaries inland waterways were a source of endless wonder. John Hustler looked into the future and saw a time when a gentleman might travel "1,500 miles in his pleasure boat, with his family, and visit ten capital cities and thirty-five principal towns of England", nearly as cheaply as he could live at home.

The Leeds-Liverpool Canal, that "north-west passage through the wilds", opened up an entirely new trade route of immense importance to the whole of the West Riding. It cut Britain in two and with the aid of navigable rivers linked the North and Irish Seas. Whoever supplied the original idea there is no doubt that the driving force was John Hustler. From the formation of the Canal Company he was the most active member of the committee, and the necessary powers were obtained from Parliament largely through his efforts. Besides all this, his outstanding position enabled him to enlist the support of influential people, many of them fellow Quakers.

For twenty-five years, part of the time as sole treasurer, Hustler devoted his entire energies to the Company's affairs. He thought six years would be enough to see the scheme completed, but the early progress was not maintained, and although more than half the canal was in operation when he died, the final link was not made until 1816.

Under the headline "Navigation between East and West Seas" the *Leeds Intelligencer* had, in June 1766, announced a meeting in Bradford at the house of Mr John Day, "known by the name of the 'Sign of the Sun' "—the old Sun Inn—to consider how best to get the canal started.

The initial meeting was held in Bradford; the chief promoter and a large number of the shareholders were Bradfordians; the head office of the Company was in Bradford until 1850, and yet Bradford was not mentioned in the original proposals. The canal was to pass within three miles of the town, but could not go through it because the hills to the north and east were too high.

Men like John Hustler and his partner Edmund Peckover, also a Quaker, were not to be beaten by a few small hills, however. In 1770 a Leeds–Liverpool Canal Company was formed and in the following year an application from Bradford was granted "for making a navigable cut or Canal from Bradford to join the Leeds and Liverpool Canal at Windhill".

Work began on the main canal, and on 8 April 1773 the bells rang out to signal the opening of the Skipton to Bingley section, the first Yorkshire stretch of the "Grand Canal", an occasion celebrated with bonfires, illuminations and two-boat-loads of cheap coal. Bradford's branch canal was to be a three-mile "navigable cut" (local people still talk about "jumping into t'cut" when they are angry) rising 86ft by ten locks, from 238ft at Windhill to 324ft at the Bradford end. And when the main canal had been extended from Bingley to Thackley the Bradford Canal made a junction with it.

The opening of the Bradford Canal in 1774 filled the town's cup of prosperity to the brim, and James Hartley could barely restrain himself as he called down blessings on the industrious poor and the merchants who, to their credit it seems, lived like noblemen. The canal and the Piece Hall, would, he said, under the Divine Blessing, prove a great and permanent benefit to every individual. 1774 was, indeed, a crucial year in Bradford's development. Some see it as the "take off": the slow gathering of momentum before the rapid expansion of the machine age.

Abraham Balme, one of the chief agents of the Bradford Navigation—the Canal Company—spent 7 September 1774, as his diary tells us, down at the canal basin in Bradford, loading up the *Good Intent* with "150 load of the better-bed coal and 100 load of the worse". The fact that one horse could pull fifty to sixty tons on the water reduced the price of coal by half, one of the immediate benefits of the new form of transport. Mr Balme followed the boat down the canal as far as the Elm Tree Inn, where three days later he sold the coal to Ben Barber. This was the measure of progress: 250 loads of coal delivered and sold, not exactly at a stroke, but within a few days.

The new waterways soon gave Bradford direct communication with the North Sea through Leeds and Hull, and later with the Irish Sea, through Liverpool. Barges brought large quantities of limestone cheaply from the Skipton district for use in smelting at Bowling and Low Moor Iron Works, a contribution which helped to make them famous throughout the world. Coal, stone and iron castings went out: limestone, agricultural produce, and occasional German pianos, we are told, came in.

"Who . . . would have believed", said Hartley, "had they been told but a few years ago, that they should live to see so wonderful, delightful, and useful a vehicle as a boat, riding upon the waves, spreading her sails to the wind, and waving her pendants in the air, in that field so many years known by the name of *Hall-Garth*: I say, who would have believed it?"

Who would have believed that seventy years later the Rev Joshua Fawcett would be saying,

The Bradford Canal was commenced in 1774. It would be a great blessing to this town if the canal could be dried up!

Why? The answer lies with the beck. From the start water had been drawn from it to feed the canal basin near Kirkgate, but the pleasant stream in which trout once swam had become a laughing-stock—T'mucky beck.

Deposits of grease from thousands of tons of wool processed at this time threatened the very existence of the town and its people. The mills which grew up near the beck repaid its kind services by pumping into it all their effluence, as much as fifty tons a day in busy times. To make matters worse, householders piled refuse on its banks, and scavenging animals nosed about in the mud. And when the beck was not a disease-ridden quagmire it was flooding the town.

6. ON THE VERGE OF THE INDUSTRIAL REVOLUTION

Bradford's increasing population at the end of the eighteenth century was housed mainly on the north side of the beck, where workers' cottages were erected in random groups called "folds", without any regard for order. Upper floors were often used both as children's bedrooms and, if father was a weaver or a comber, as workshops.

A feature of most downstairs rooms—referred to in the West Riding as "the house"—was a shut-up bed in which the parents usually slept. By day this was a piece of furniture which looked like a wardrobe or cupboard, but by night the front let down to disclose a ready-made bed.

There was, as yet, no gas, so all lighting was by oil or candles. Water was drawn from a pump or well. Food was plain, with plenty of oatmeal for porridge and for the oat-cakes which hung close to the ceiling, either on laths or on a drying line thrown across the room. In large families it was usually a case of, "Them 'at eats most pudding can 'ave most meat", for joints were scarce.

Bradford was then served by no more than four or five stage coaches, which halted at their respective inns before climbing the hills on their outward journey. The "Highflyer", the "Union" and the "Mail" thundered down Church Bank along Kirkgate, and down Ivegate, on their way from Leeds into Lancashire, but the steep climb uphill, on the return, was a different matter. By 1825 fourteen coaches were running daily to and from Leeds, and it was because the journey up Church Bank proved so difficult that the new Leeds Road was made, the two running parallel until they joined at Thornbury, two miles from the town.

A market barely worthy of the name was held in Westgate, around the cross which has since found a home in the grounds of Bolling Hall. A more regular kind of market was accommodated in a strange building designed, so it was said, according to a plan brought back from Italy by William Rawson, lord of the manor. The Old Market Hall, which also served as assembly rooms, Sunday School, and even as a temporary barracks, stood on the site of the Wool Exchange, giving Market Street (formerly New Street) its name. The Piece Hall was nearby and a little further up Kirkgate, on the opposite side, was the Manor Hall.

Across the Beck, near Sun Bridge, was the town's recreation ground, Turles. Here there was a bowling green, and in what little leisure time they had, men could play knur and spell or wager on an arrow throwing contest. The old Cockpit building had been given over to better uses, one large room having been let to the Methodists in 1756, but they soon left the "Synagogue of Satan" for the new Octagon Chapel in Horton Lane.

John Wesley, who was always pleased to visit Bradford, preached at the Cockpit in 1757. He had special praise for "the largest Octagon in England . . . the first of its kind where the roof is built with common sense"; but in spite of Wesley's admiration for it the new chapel was structurally unsound and only lasted forty years.

The forces of strict religion in the town were very strong, but not nearly strong enough to counteract the evils which spread from fifty or more public houses, a situation which caused a local poet, William Darney, to write:

> On Bradford likewise look Thou down,
>   Where Satan keeps his seat;
> Come, by Thy power: Lord! him dethrone,
>   For Thou art very great.

In 1797 the safety of Bradford's six thousand inhabitants was in the hands of two constables, always important men chosen by the Manor Courts. They in turn appointed several deputy constables to do the work of policemen, but as their contracts did not include night duty, those who wanted protection during the hours of darkness subscribed to a fund from which six watchmen were paid, on condition that they only "watched" property belonging to subscribers. Until the formation of the Bradford Gas Light Company in 1821 the streets were lit by widely spaced oil lamps, and the valiant six, equipped with lanterns and rattles, patrolled their beats from huts, calling the hours as they went. Of course, the outer townships, Horton and Bowling, had to police their own districts.

Justice in the West Riding was administered by magistrates who held Quarter Sessions at various towns in turn, Bradford being one of them; and besides punishing criminals they issued licences to publicans, settled rates of wages and attended to such things as the maintenance of roads and bridges. Petty Sessions were often held near towns, so that when all offenders had been dealt with local matters could be discussed.

The ordinary people made their voices heard at vestry meetings, which could be called by any two ratepayers, a notice being pinned to the door of the Parish Church and read out on Sundays. Although the vestry had considerable powers, the meetings were often poorly attended and inefficiently conducted. There was little public spirit abroad because the ratepayers were simply content to guard their own interests, and progress came to a standstill.

Bradford was then severely troubled by straying pigs, and when an order forbidding owners to allow this had been ignored the vestry resolved:

> that public notice be given by the cryer and by handbills that . . . the owner of such pig or pigs as are found at large will be indicted for the same by the constable of the town.

A reward of a shilling was also offered to any person who brought a straying pig to justice.

Lack of sanitation caused frequent epidemics in the town and in 1799, when fever broke out, food was scarce because of bad harvests. The result was much suffering, and death in almost every home. At this time the Rev. John Crosse was Vicar of Bradford and an account tells how, regardless of his health, he went from house to house, day and night, visiting the sick and providing them with food, blankets and other necessities. In many a "lost, filthy dwelling", where no restoration seemed possible, he personally superintended the cleansing of it.

Towards the end of his life John Crosse became blind and had to be led by the hand as he went about his duties, a little boy or girl usually accompanying him.

As Bradford grew, problems of water supply, cleansing and maintaining order—all that we now call social services—proved too much for such organisation as there was, and some far-sighted people petitioned Parliament for an Act to empower them to improve the town. This "Act for Paving, Lighting, Watching and Improving the town of Bradford, and part of the hamlet of Little Horton adjoining thereto . . ." was passed in 1803 and authorised fifty-eight men known as Commissioners, who must not be victuallers or sell ale, to carry out the provisions of the Act. They also had to supply fire engines and to see that the mill chimneys were high enough to allow smoke to get away.

The Commissioners gradually increased the number of watchmen to thirty-eight, and also made arrangements with the Bradford Gas Light Company to light the streets. Otherwise the new brooms did not sweep very clean. The roads were in a very bad state, Chapel Lane being described as "totally impassable except on stilts", and one report declared that people who went out were "doomed to wade through seas of sludge to the imminent risk of their lives and limbs".

Like other industrial towns Bradford, as it increased in size, deteriorated. Many of the workers' homes were mere hovels, where one room accomodated a family of either four or ten.

F

Small wonder that half the children died before reaching the age of five; but even those who were better housed fared as badly. George Lumb, landlord of the Old Crown, Ivegate, married his wife, Elizabeth, in 1800, and of their seven children only one survived infancy.

So, as the full force of the Industrial Revolution was about to hit Bradford, the people discovered that they needed more than just "Bread and Peace". The town, with its population of thirteen thousand, was utterly unequipped to deal with the sudden influx of families, and its rising prosperity must be seen against a background of misery and suffering.

In the sixteenth century, when York was losing its clothing trade to the West Riding, a writer explained:

> for that not only the comodytie of the water mylnes is ther nigh at hande, but also the poore folke as speynners, carders and other necessary workfolkes.

Water and "poore folke" were indeed a beginning, but Bradford had other resources, too.

Coal had been mined in the district since the Middle Ages, but there was no great demand for it until machinery came into use. Then abundant supplies of cheap coal were ready to hand; and when metal was needed to replace wooden machines, ironstone, from which the Low Moor Company produced "Best Yorkshire", was only forty yards below the surface.

In addition, the surrounding hills contained fine sandstone, which was waiting to be quarried; so that all building, from the smallest cottage to the largest new factory, was in local stone. Bricks were only used for inner walls and even the roofs of houses were made of flat thackstones.

The raw materials were at hand: coal, iron, and stone; and families from near and far were ready to move into the district when the least chance of employment was offered to them.

Last, but by no means least, Bradford's "useful men", the

captains of industry, were there to supply the capital and take command of affairs.

Leland, in his description of Bradford, spoke of "a confluence in the toune of three brokes". The main stream was, of course, the Bradford Beck: the other two, neither of which can be seen now, flowed from Bowling and Bradford Moor. Tributaries to the beck used to flow from all parts of the bowl in which Bradford lies, and at one time the valley must have sparkled with rivulets. Now, many of them have either dried up or been directed into culverts. The remaining open streams come from the hills to the west, from Thornton, Clayton and Allerton; and at Middle Brook, where Bull Royd Syke joins them, the stream becomes Bradford Beck.

In Bradford the influence of geography upon history is very marked, because this little stream—T'mucky beck—is at the heart of the city's development, from a small country town to the centre of the world's wool textile industry. But few Bradfordians have ever seen their native stream, for it goes underground at Brownroyd, runs beneath the city centre, and doesn't emerge until it is well on the way to join the River Aire at Shipley.

In earlier times the beck supplied the town with drinking water, provided the power to turn the mill wheels and was the essential means of wool washing, fulling and dyeing. Water from the beck was diverted into a goit which ran from Water Lane, across Thornton Road and along Goit Side until it reached the corn mill in Aldermanbury, after which it returned to the main stream. Near Ingleby Road a dam was made to keep the goit running swiftly.

Yet, by strange paradox, it was Bradford's *lack* of water, its natural disadvantages once again, which turned the attention of manufacturers to the possibilities of steam. Unlike Halifax, Bradford had never committed itself very heavily to water-powered mills, so manufacturers in the town were free to invest wholeheartedly in steam engines.

When "steam ousted stream" the becks, contrarily, became

more indispensable than ever. Not only was the soft moorland water needed at every stage of wool processing; it also became a new source of power, a means of steam raising for boilers and generators. Some wise factory owners sank their own wells and assured themselves of inexhaustible supplies. Those who didn't adopt this policy had to wait for independence from the becks until piped water was made available.

An indication of the absolute importance of water may be gained from the correspondence between Sir Francis Lindley Wood and his agent, concerning the sale of a plot of land for a factory near Claw Beck Bridge in Bowling. Claw Beck, usually called Law Beck, separated the townships of Bowling and Horton.

In 1814 Richard Smith of Horton applied for a site in this neighbourhood, but fears were expressed that the supply to the Bowling Corn Mill would be affected if water were drawn off higher up the stream. However, Isaac Wells, the agent, wrote most strongly to his employer, saying:

> Now, Sir, you must consider that water is the first and principal moving cause, and the only one . . . of the place being chosen for erecting the intended engine and factory.

He went on to explain that the difficulty could be overcome by returning the water to the stream, less the amount evaporated, after it had served its purpose. And so Dick Smith got his mill in Bowling Old Lane, on or near the site later occupied by Mitchell Brothers' mill.

In spite of its importance the Bradford Beck was not an unmixed blessing. During heavy storms it became overcharged and caused spectacular floods in the dale. One Sunday morning in 1768 large quantities of wool and cloth were carried away by the beck, and a man and a boy standing on Kirk Bridge were drowned. In 1822 Benjamin Baines, a druggist, was swept away while examining a water-mark which he had set up outside his house; and his body was not found until three days afterwards. On a later occasion a man was said to have rowed a boat along Market Street.

If water was the "first and principal moving cause", coal was the second, and when coal was needed there was no dearth of it in Bradford.

Beneath the town there were two coal seams; the lower *Better Bed*, at a depth of about eighty yards, resting on a hard sandstone called *galliard*; the higher *Black Bed*, forty yards or so from the surface, lying immediately below a layer of rock containing valuable ironstone.

The great demand for coal began when iron machines replaced wooden ones, and increased by leaps and bounds when mills were powered by steam. Soon Bradford was ringed round by pits, and horse-drawn wagons ran on wooden rails to various staiths in the town. Later these tracks were replaced by "Iron Roads", and the Low Moor district was criss-crossed by a network of railways to and from the pits owned by the Company, at one time as many as seventy *Better Bed* pits alone. Of course, these were not pits as we understand them today. Many of them were small concerns employing only a few men, and some were "day holes", that is, without shafts.

Before iron was mined in Low Moor, Squire Leedes ran a flourishing coal business and the tramways he laid ran from Little Horton, Wibsey and Royds Hall to Colliergate, not far from the canal basin. Some of the coal was sold in the town, but many thousands of loads were shipped at the nearby canal wharf. The Low Moor Company owned most of the land in the Wibsey–Little Horton area, where there were two coal staiths, one near the Old Black Horse Inn and the other where Brigella Mills now stand.

Iron and coal went hand in hand. Once Bradford realized the value of its mineral deposits foundries were established, five being in operation by 1811. Emmetts, who opened at Birkenshaw in 1782 were the pioneers, with Bowling Iron Works and the Low Moor Company not far behind.

Many of the greatest industrial concerns begin in the unlikeliest places, and from the Upper Independent Chapel at Idle, where he was more successful as a farmer and mine owner than as a minister or schoolmaster, the Rev. Joseph

Dawson emerged to found the Low Moor Company. Dawson was a remarkable man, but his pursuit of worldly affairs, we are told, led him into such eccentricities as using the chapel as a storage place for cattle fodder and keeping poultry among the gravestones.

The other partners in the Company were Richard Hird, woolstapler, John Jarratt, draper, and John Hardy, solicitor. Hardy, one of the protestors against the likely pollution from Mr Buckley's proposed steam mill in Bradford, now gave his backing to a foundry which was soon to cover the countryside with huge slag heaps.

Joseph Dawson was the only partner with any scientific knowledge. He had studied at Glasgow University, where he became acquainted with James Watt, and he also struck up a friendship with Dr Joseph Priestley of Birstall. The decision to buy Royds Hall Estate, Low Moor, was only made after consultation with Dr Priestley, upon which Dawson took possession of Royds Hall, the Manor House, and settled down to business. From that point he devoted his many talents to the affairs of the Company, but showed that he had not entirely forgotten his pastoral duties by opening a Day and Sunday School in 1791. In that year the first blast engine, made at Emmetts, came into use, and the Low Moor Company went on to celebrate its centenary.

The Company began by manufacturing wheels, rails and miscellaneous articles, but in addition was soon supplying the country with armaments of all kinds. Henceforward, at battles on land and sea, at Trafalgar, Waterloo and in the Crimea, "Best Yorkshire", as Low Moor Iron was called, did its duty. During the Crimean War the production was almost entirely given over to smelting iron for guns, mortars and cannon balls.

"Best Yorkshire" was the result of an ideal partnership between the almost sulphur-free Better Bed coal and ironstone with a very low phosphorous content. It was this combination which produced the iron on which Low Moor's world wide renown was founded. Bowling Iron Works was somewhat overshadowed by Low Moor, but it was a large concern which also enjoyed a high international reputation.

In the spate of building during the nineteenth century in Bradford local quarries played their part, supplying an abundance of stone for factories and houses, as well as flags and cobbles for the streets. Stones for the early town were obtained from Ivegate and Westgate, but as Bradford expanded the old workings were covered over and built upon. Many central buildings occupy these sites and maps show that John Street Market stands on Coppy Quarry, which was still in operation in 1832. Gradually more and more quarries opened up on the outskirts of the town, to the north, south and west, until there were more than forty altogether.

The major outcrop in the surrounding hills consisted of "Elland flags", an all purpose stone, which was used for roads, pavements, walls, and roofs. Few places could count themselves so fortunately placed for building materials as Bradford. In fact, the town became such a good advertisement for local stone that Tong Hall was the only brick building of any consequence in the whole district.

Quarries along the beck, to the north, benefited from the opening of the canals, and from Cliffe Wood, Spinkwell and Greencliffe stone was shipped for the Customs House at Liverpool and for use in the construction of Manchester Town Hall. The really heavy demand for local stone came after 1850, and twenty years later, at the peak period, almost 450,000 tons a year were being sold by Bradford quarry owners.

One thing Bradford needed as it entered the Machine Age was access to large supplies of good quality wool, and it was a local man, Samuel Marsden of Farsley, who introduced West Riding manufacturers to Botany Bay wool.

When the Rev. Samuel Marsden presented himself in audience at Windsor Castle, wearing a new suit of sober black, George III is said to have admired it and to have asked for a coat of the same cloth, a request readily granted. The cloth had been woven at Rawdon, a few miles from Bradford. The wearer, who was chaplain to the convict settlement in New

South Wales, had brought the wool back with him, the first consignment of Australian wool—a mere 165 pounds—to reach Yorkshire.

The call to the ministry had come to young Sam Marsden as he worked in a blacksmith's shop at Horsforth. After studying at home he went to Hull Grammar School and then to Cambridge, but in 1792, before he took his degree, a post in the Government chaplaincy was offered to him. The next year saw him ordained, married and on his way to Australia. The Marsdens, father, mother and daughter Anne, landed at Sydney on 10 March 1794, from where they moved on to Parramatta and set up home in the barracks. Not long after their arrival the senior chaplain resigned, leaving Mr Marsden in charge of the spiritual affairs of the settlement.

A Government grant of a hundred acres of land and five convicts to do the work established him in agriculture. Within a few years he became an authority on sheep breeding and, along with Captain John MacArthur of the New South Wales Corps, Marsden is credited with founding the great Australian wool growing industry.

When Captain Bligh of the Bounty was made Governor of New South Wales a crisis arose, and Marsden came home to report to the British Government. The ship on which the family sailed sprang a leak and they were asked to transfer to another vessel. They refused in order to stand by the invalid wife of a former Governor, but as the other ship sank, the good deed saved their lives. It also saved the barrels of Botany Bay wool from which the cloth for Samuel Marsden's suit and King George's coat were made.

Captain MacArthur had already bought several Merino sheep from the Royal Farm at Kew. The King now insisted on sending back with the Marsdens a gift of five Merino ewes with young, as a gift to the Colony. In this small way an industry was founded on which Bradford's fortunes were to be built. In 1813 Mr Marsden sent eight thousand pounds of Botany wool to England, the bulk of it for Bradford's mills. The Rt. Rev. S E Marsden, Lord Bishop of Bathurst, Samuel

Marsden's grandson, said that many years after the wool landed he actually spoke to a Leeds man who unpacked the consignment. Botany Bay wool became so much a part of the Bradford trade that it was referred to, not as wool, but simply as botany.

Samuel Marsden had long wished to preach to the Maoris of New Zealand, but it was not until 1814 that his ambition was fulfilled. The first Christian service was held on land owned by Chief Ruatara, a Maori who had been befriended by Mr Marsden on the return journey from England. Samuel Marsden became known as the "Apostle of New Zealand" and at Farsley he is well remembered, with memorial windows in the church, a monument in the churchyard and commemorative tablets on a wall near the place where he was born.

7. EARLY DAYS OF THE INDUSTRIAL REVOLUTION

Lancashire was the birthplace of new ideas which led to the Industrial Revolution, and three inventions in the space of a few years sent cotton production soaring.

The first and perhaps least spectacular invention, in 1733, was John Kay's flying shuttle, so called because it was smacked backwards and forwards across the loom at great speed. The movement of the shuttle was controlled by cords held in the weaver's right hand, so that he always had one hand free to beat the weft threads up. Before this, spinners were hard pressed to supply all the yarn needed by weavers, but now they fell further behind. James Hargreaves solved the problem in 1767 by producing a machine which would spin several threads simultaneously. His jenny, with eight spindles, was a great success and in its final form took as many as a hundred and twenty spindles.

Richard Arkwright, a Preston wigmaker, patented a spinning frame driven by water in 1769, and two years later these machines were working in a mill at Cromford in Derbyshire. Samuel Crompton combined the best features of the jenny and the water frame in a spinning mule, which produced finer yarns than ever before. This machine was entirely automatic by 1830. James Watt discovered the use of steam in 1765, and from a mere toy developed an engine which changed the habits of a whole nation.

The least likely inventor-to-be was Edmund Cartwright, country parson and poet who, as he dined at Matlock in the summer of 1784, overheard a group of Lancashire manufacturers discussing spinning jennies. They expressed fears that if these machines were made in unlimited numbers there would be more yarn than weavers could use, and disaster would follow. To their surprise Cartwright joined in the conversation, stating emphatically that things must be altered. Then, without the slightest knowledge of textile machinery, he went away to show the world how it could be done. In 1785 he patented the power loom, a clumsy contrivance scarcely recognizable in later developments. By 1815 power looms were in fairly general use in Lancashire, and before the middle of the century cotton provided half our exports and a quarter of all imports.

The West Riding was slow to admit the claims of machinery, and in 1793 when an "enterprising gentleman" called Buckley had the effrontery to propose to build a mill at the bottom of Manchester Road, in the heart of Bradford's Town End, he was firmly put in his place by the residents, who served a notice on him, saying:

> if either you or any person in connexion with you shall presume to erect or build any steam-engine for the manufacture of cotton or wool, in a certain field in Horton, near Bradford, aforesaid, called or known by the name of the Brick-kiln Field, we whose names are hereunto subscribed shall, if the same be found a nuisance, seek such redress as the law will give.

In the face of this threat Mr Buckley did not build his mill, but having stopped him it is somewhat significant, that several of those who signed the notice took a leading part afterwards in erecting "objectionable mill chimneys".

John Hustler died too early to see the introduction of machinery in Bradford, but when he and James Garnett met on the Worsted Committee, the latter would be sure to discuss the plans he had for installing spinning machines at his fine country house, Paper Hall, at the top of Church Bank. The second floor became a workshop, and in 1794 two of these machines, mules and throstle, were worked there by hand.

At about the same time Robert Ramsbotham, to his regret,

took one of Mr Cartwright's combing machines into his premises at Kirkgate, where it was turned by a horse in a gin. The machine was a complete failure, and onlookers reported that a sadder and wiser Mr Ramsbotham was seen to raise his hat as "Big Ben" was carted away.

When three partners with the good old Yorkshire names of Ramsbotham, Swaine and Murgatroyd began to erect Bradford's first spinning mill they encountered considerable opposition. One partner even had to show fight in order to clear a way for the wagons carrying building materials to the site, near where the Alhambra now stands. *The Holme*, with its 15 horse power engine, was completed in 1800, but four years later the Volunteers were called to deal with a fire which almost destroyed it. Save for the trouble at *The Holme* the masters met with little opposition, but in parts of the West Riding, where Luddites went about smashing machinery, there were great outbreaks of violence.

The Luddites took their name from "General" Ned Ludd, the leader of Nottinghamshire gangs who went round destroying knitting machines which they felt were threatening their means of livelihood. In Yorkshire there were attacks on the machines which were putting hand shearers—the men who dressed the cloth—out of work. Some of these machines were made by a Marsden man called Enoch Taylor, who was also a manufacturer of hammers. With grim humour the wreckers christened the hammer they used "Enoch", and the war cry became "Enoch has made 'em; Enoch shall break 'em".

In 1812 a mob marched on Rawfolds Mill, Liversedge, but the owner of the factory, William Cartwright, was armed and ready when they arrived. With the help of a few soldiers and workmen he beat off the attack, killing two men; a deed for which he received a testimonial of £3,000 from other mill owners. This incident was used by Charlotte Bronte in her novel *Shirley*.

By way of revenge Luddites attacked a clothier called William Horsfall as he made his way from Huddersfield over Crosland Moor, and for this crime three men were hanged at

York. This incident also finds its way into a West Riding novel, Phyllis Bentley's *Inheritance*.

There was comparative peace in the Bradford district until 1822, when James Warbrick had a power loom secretly made and smuggled into a mill at Shipley. The news leaked out and the factory was soon surrounded by a mob of angry weavers, who threatened to destroy the building unless the loom was removed. Mr Warbrick accordingly dismantled the loom, placed it on a cart and, with an escort of constables, began to move it away. The weavers, now out of control, attacked the cart, routed the constables and broke up the loom. Having done this they dragged the warp and rollers through Baildon in triumph.

There was no rush to build factories in Bradford, but John Rand, an objector to Buckley's proposal, erected one in 1803, and by 1810 there were at least five—all spinning mills. Once the initial opposition had been overcome building went on at the rate of about one factory a year and families moved into the town to provide the labour force. In 1831 there were thirty-one factories, mostly given over to spinning, and the population had risen from 13,264 in 1801 to 43,527.

Most of the factory workers were women and children, men being occupied at home, either as handloom weavers or hand-combers. It was very useful to have children who could supplement the family income, and boys and girls were pushed out into the spinning mills as soon as the employers would take them. Bad as this system was, it gave a stability of a sort and formed the pattern of life in Bradford until about 1838, when power looms began to throw large numbers of hand-weavers out of work. There was a further big upheaval with the invention of the combing machine, which put an end to home industry by 1850.

Once every seven years masters and men in Bradford took a day off work to keep the festival of St Blaize, the last and most splendid commemoration being that of 1825.

One of the key figures in the pageant was Richard Fawcett

Handloom

—"King Richard"—also known as the "Founder of the Worsted Trade", who lived in a house in historic Hunt Yard. After building a worsted spinning mill in Union Street Mr Fawcett bought and rebuilt *The Holme*. He then left Great Horton, where he employed a large number of hand-loom weavers, for Westbrook House, a site since occupied by the Alexandra Hotel. He died in 1845 leaving, we are told, a good name to his children, but no great wealth.

Few things can be stranger than Bradford's association with an obscure Armenian bishop, who, according to tradition, was martyred in Sebaste in the year AD 316. St Blaize—Blase or Blazius—is said to have been tortured by means of iron combs, and put to death, since when legends about him have multiplied, each one more remarkable than the last. The instruments of his martyrdom made him the patron saint of woolcombers, and Bradford did him special honour.

By seven o'clock on the morning of 3 February 1825 strangers from twenty miles around were coming into Bradford to line the route of the procession. Never had the town known such crowds. An hour later representatives of the different trades began to assemble at the Bull's Head in Westgate, but it was quite ten o'clock before they were ready to move off.

The procession, led by a Herald bearing a flag, was in magnificent array, the order being:

Herald

24 Woolstaplers on horseback, each horse caparisoned with a fleece.

38 Worsted spinners and Manufacturers on horseback, in white stuff waistcoats . . . the horses' necks covered with nets made of thick yarn.

6 Merchants on horseback with coloured sashes. . . .

56 Apprentices and Masters' sons, on horseback, with ornamented caps, scarlet stuff coats, white stuff waistcoats and blue pantaloons.

The next contingent, headed by the Bradford and Keighley Bands, included Bishop Blaize and his Chaplain. Before the Bishop went the King and Queen with an escort of Guards, and behind him walked a Shepherd, Shepherdess and Swains.

Six or seven hundred workers made up the body of the procession:

160 Woolsorters on horseback, with ornamented caps and various coloured slivers.

30 Combmakers

Charcoal burners. . . .

And after another band came 470 Woolcombers wearing wool wigs. 40 Dyers brought up the rear, looking very splendid in their red cockades, blue aprons and crossed slivers of red and blue. The workers who stole the picture, however, were the apprentices,

their caps being richly adorned with ostrich feathers, flowers and knots of various coloured yarn, and their stuff garments being of the gayest colours; some of these dresses, we understand, were very costly from the profusion of their decorations.

The head-dresses of the woolsorters, tall, gaily coloured plumes in the shape of fleur-de-lis, gave them a dashing appearance, while the woolcombers carried the instruments of torture raised on standards, together with golden fleeces, rams' heads and gilded horns.

The signal to march came when "King Richard", on horseback at the head of the spinners pronounced, "uncovered and with great animation" the customary lines:

> *"Hail to the day, whose kind auspicious rays*
> *Deign'd first to smile on famous Bishop Blaize:"*

words which were repeated several times at different places.

The cavalcade, almost a mile long, went via Kirkgate, Ivegate, Market Street and Horton Lane to a field near Holme Mill, where abundant refreshments were provided. One writer tells how, as a little boy, he sat on his father's shoulders watching the barrels of ale being tapped and men walking about "with enormous sandwiches in their hands, shivering with the cold, bleak February wind". His account ends with the sad reflection that as the day resulted in drunkenness and disorder it was a good thing the festival was stopped. To Titus Salt and the others it was merely a relic of barbarous times.

There was a brief revival, with a procession in 1857, and the Church Steps Society, formed by workers to uphold the festival, kept memories alive at an annual dinner held in the Church Steps Inn on 3 February, the Saint's anniversary. Two inns once bore his name, the Bishop Blaize in Kirkgate and the Old Bishop Blaize in Westgate, but these have now disappeared.

Few reminders of the Saint's connection with Bradford remain, but his statue, comb in hand, keeps watch at the entrance to the Wool Exchange, along with a King who is believed to be Edward III. The hand-made clothes worn by Richard Fawcett at the St Blaize festival have been preserved and are kept in Bolling Hall. There is a carved figure of St Blaize over the Provost's stall in the Cathedral and, more recently, a school has been named after him.

In February 1825 Richard Fawcett had proclaimed the town's gratitude to "the great author of our combing trade" for his goodness to the poor, but by June he would have risked being pelted for reciting:

> By this our trade are thousands daily fed;
> By it supplied with means to earn their bread.

This was precisely the trouble: men couldn't earn enough to buy their daily bread. The beer and sandwiches of February were forgotten by June, when many families were facing starvation.

The woolcombers and handloom weavers went on strike for higher wages and together held out for nearly six months. This was the most disastrous time the town had experienced since the Civil War, and it appeared all the more unpleasant because in the previous year the whole country had enjoyed good trade. The banks had plenty of money to lend and South America, "the land of the future", attracted speculators.

Unfortunately, by the end of 1825 there was panic as it became known that the expected profits on South American investments were not forthcoming. London was in a state of commotion. In less than three weeks seventy-three banks failed, among them Wentworth, Rishworth and Chaloner's, which had a branch in Bradford. The only other Bradford bank, the Old Bank, founded by Edmund Peckover of Eastbrook House, in partnership with his nephew Charles Harris, weathered the storm. But this crisis, together with the strike, brought business to a standstill.

In November, with hundreds of families without a wage earner, not only famine but disease and sickness threatened the town. Fortunately there was a good deal of sympathy for the strikers and their dependants. The Vicar of Bradford, the Rev. Henry Heap, headed a band of volunteers who gave timely help. Large sums of money were collected and in one week alone nearly seventy tons of oatmeal and flour were distributed to two thousand families.

This was not the end of the task, for the sick needed atten-

G

tion and it had already been decided to establish a dispensary "for the use of the indigent poor". Almost all the money for this venture came from voluntary efforts or direct gifts. James Ellis and Company, the occupiers of the Soke Mills, offered all the fines levied upon their customers, and the editor of the *Bradford Courier* handed over the proceeds of his lecture on "Phrenology".

The Bradford Royal Infirmary, which rose from these small beginnings, had its origins in a house owned by Charles Harris the banker, at the junction of Peckover Street with High Street. The Old Dispensary served its immediate purpose, but the building was quite inadequate and new premises were opened in Darley Street two years later.

As the woolcombers' and handloom weavers' strike dragged on allegations were made by both sides. The employers said that a comber's wage, on average, was twenty-five shillings a week, while the men claimed that this amount was only arrived at by adding the earnings of wives and children who helped them. Realizing that they had little chance of success many combers disobeyed their union and returned to work, risking whatever violence might result. Three men and a woman, who molested a William Ryan because he had accepted work from Mr Fawcett, were sent to the House of Correction at Wakefield.

The woolcombers issued a manifesto informing the public that their occupation was the sure way to "an untimely grave" and that wives who helped in such an unhealthy atmosphere aged rapidly. The manifesto was impassioned and highly emotional, but in stressing the unpleasant nature of their calling the men were not exaggerating. The air in the bedrooms, for that is where they usually worked, was thick with fumes from the charcoal stoves in which the combs were heated.

It was an arduous job, too, for the heavy T-shaped combs contained up to a hundred and twenty long steel teeth. The teeth of the combs were heated in the "pot", which usually held four combs, and then one of them was fastened to a large post called a pad-post and a handful of oiled wool was placed on the hot teeth. Then another comb was drawn through the wool, unravelling the fibres and laying them out smooth and straight. The whole process was carried on in an atmosphere heavy with oily vapour and charcoal fumes.

The woolcombers also tried to arouse feeling against the masters by describing the sufferings of children who worked in the mills. But in spite of all, the strikers failed and were compelled to return to work on the same terms as before. Their union, described as "an efficient instrument for harm", proved itself incapable of matching the power of the employers, and was dissolved. The most savage blow of all came when it was learnt that the treasurer, John Tester, had absconded with the funds.

The strike was over, but peace did not last long. There were serious riots the following year, when power looms were installed at Horsfalls' mill in North Wing, not far from Paper Hall. On 1 May 1826, soon after the arrival of the machines, a crowd of about two hundred and fifty unemployed men gathered at Fairweather Green where, after some discussion, a decision was made to attack the mill.

Late in the afternoon the marchers reached North Wing, and staged a demonstration in which six windows were broken. Unable to do any further damage the men, now hungry and frustrated, moved on to Bradford Moor where they were joined by two hundred others. In the evening the combined force returned to mount a second attack. At the height of the stone throwing, during which many more windows were broken, an army of special constables arrived and the mob dispersed.

All this happened on Monday. On Wednesday another meeting, much larger than before, was held at Fairweather Green and again the men, in a much more determined mood, set off for Horsfalls' mill. Here the owners had worked quickly to prepare for a siege by replacing the broken panes, fastening iron bars across the windows and securing the doors by means of thick planks.

About a hundred defenders, some equipped with pistols and small arms, stood ready to repulse the attack, which began at four in the afternoon. For about half an hour the factory withstood a barrage of stones, during which three window frames were completely destroyed, but no one succeeded in making an entry. The disturbances were quelled for a time by the arrival of a force of special constables headed by Colonel Plumbe Tempest, who read the Riot Act from a piece of spare ground nearby.

In spite of this the mob showed no signs of disbanding. The stone throwing began again, and the attack might have petered out if someone in the crowd had not fired a pistol into the mill. The defenders retaliated, firing several volleys into the crowd and killing two young people, one of them a boy of thirteen called Edward Fearnley. Many others were wounded. This brought the sad day to an unhappy end, as a result of which two of the rioters were sent to York Castle.

8. "YORKSHIRE SLAVERY" AND RIOTS

The nineteenth century is sometimes called "The Century of the Child", because of the efforts made to rescue children from slavery in factories and educate them. The inhuman treatment of the factory children, which the woolcombers wished to make known, is one of the saddest stories in all British history. Bradford children suffered more than most, and it is a credit to the town that it had men of conscience, like John Wood and the Rev. G S Bull, who were prepared to fight to end a national scandal. It was Richard Oastler, however, who set the campaign in motion.

One night in September 1830 Richard Oastler, a land agent of Fixby, near Huddersfield, went to Horton Hall to see his friend John Wood, who owned two large spinning mills in Bradford. Oastler was a very busy man, but among all his commitments found time to open a school on his estate and also to take an active part in the campaign to end the Slave Trade.

As they talked in the firelight, Wood asked Oastler why, among all his good works, he had never done anything to put an end to the evils of the factory system. Oastler, clearly surprised, said that factories were no concern of his. The mill owner then gave an account of the cruelties inflicted upon the children of Bradford, a denunciation which made Oastler both astounded and ashamed that he had remained so long in ignorance of such ill treatment.

Early the next morning Oastler found his host reading the Bible and, as they said good-bye, Wood made him promise to help the factory children. With his hand on the Bible, Oastler made a solemn vow that he would do all he could.

That night he wrote a letter to the *Leeds Mercury*, the first of many, calling upon all God-fearing men to end "Yorkshire Slavery". The letter caused a storm throughout the county and, although many manufacturers opposed Oastler violently, a few very influential people joined the campaign to shorten hours of work and make the employment of very young children illegal.

Public feeling had now been aroused and Oastler became the leader of one of the Short Time Committees formed by the workers to press for fairer conditions for themselves and their children. In 1831 a Ten Hours Bill was presented to Parliament by Michael Sadler, MP for Newark, and in 1832 in order to gain support for the Bill, "King Richard", as Oastler

Children working in a mill

was now called, planned an Easter pilgrimage to York from towns in the West Riding.

The Bradford contingent, led by "Parson Bull" of Bierley, was joined in Leeds by two columns from Halifax and Huddersfield. Just before midnight on Easter Monday the order to advance was given, but it was also the signal for a fierce thunderstorm and heavy rain. The ill-equipped, hungry pilgrims presented a pathetic spectacle as they clattered off into the darkness, waving their torches and home-made banners. At York Racecourse the rations they were expecting had not arrived, and only the appearance of the "King" himself averted mutiny. Food was distributed in the Castle Yard and, after long speeches, the solemn oath "Our children shall be free" was taken. Then, for twelve thousand tired and hungry men, the long march home began—in pouring rain. Parson Bull, to the fore again, hired coaches, kindly paid for by John Wood, picked up the stragglers and conveyed them safely on their way.

The progress of the Ten Hours Bill was halted, first by the appointment of a Select Committee and then by the General Election of 1832. Michael Sadler himself headed the Committee which enquired into the conditions under which factory children worked. Among the witnesses were several from Bradford: the Rev. G S Bull; William Sharp, the surgeon who looked after the health of children in Wood's mill; John Hall, an overlooker at Wood's, and several workpeople.

The Report was a weighty document which, even if half of it were true, amounted to damning evidence against the mill owners. Great care was taken by Oastler, who also appeared before the Committee, to see that witnesses were well briefed. The long journey to London and the cross-questioning by such an important body of people must have been a terrifying ordeal for seventeen-year-old Robert Colton, who had probably never been so far from Bradford before.

He told how, when a boy, he worked at Varley's, Stanningley, in the summer months from 3.30 in the morning until 9.30 in the evening, and said that when the "young master" died they were allowed to attend the funeral, for which 1½d was deducted from their wages. When asked "Why did you stay there?", the answer was, "We must either work or starve."

There was undoubted evidence that children were beaten, especially at the end of the day, when they were tired. Michael Sadler shocked MPs, during his speech before the Second Reading of the Bill, by producing one of the whips used. The House resounded as he brought the heavy leather strap down upon the table.

John Hall, an overlooker at Wood's mill, had the names of two hundred families with deformed children, and Richard Wilson, who worked at Matthew Thompson's mill as a boy, said he slept, or tried to sleep, with his legs fastened together from the ankles to the knees for a whole year. He had a deformed sister, who walked with a crutch, and a brother who could only get to the mill if he were carried there.

Parson Bull's evidence was based on first hand experience of children in his Sunday Schools. Describing the hours they worked, he said :

> many of my little children . . . set off regularly at five o'clock and do not return until eight almost the year round. . . . They see, therefore, very little of their parents. . . .

Some of the children in his schools, he knew, would not see the year out; and a few were so ill when he left to go before the Committee that he didn't expect to see them alive again. And of conditions in the homes, he said :

> I have frequently visited by night the cottages of the operatives for the purpose of baptizing a child that was expected to die, and have sometimes found five persons in one bed, three children lying at the feet, and their parents at the other end with the little baby between them.

Before the Report could be published, however, the first General Election after the passing of the Reform Bill took place, and Michael Sadler was defeated by Thomas Babington Macaulay, an opponent of factory legislation. It was now left to Parson Bull to approach Lord Ashley, better known to us as Shaftesbury, and ask him to put the Bill before the House again, which, after some hesitation he agreed to do.

From the amount of controversy created it might be thought that the proposed Bill was about to reduce the children's working week by half. In fact, the ten hour day was really a *twelve hour day*, including meal breaks, with eight hours on Saturday —a sixty-eight hour week for all between the ages of nine and eighteen. No child under nine was to be employed in a factory and no night work was to be done by anybody under twenty-one.

The Report of the Select Committee was published in August 1832, but Parliament decided that a Royal Commission—a more official body—should now enquire into factory conditions. For this purpose Assistant Commissioners visited the industrial towns, taking down answers to a set list of questions from both masters and men.

The Commissioners, who were suspected of being on the side of the employers, received a rough welcome in Bradford, where John Wood refused them entrance to his mill because he feared they might be insulted by the workers. Large meetings were held and children, making the occasion something of a holiday, hurled abuse at the officials, who were referred to as "the enemy". The Commissioners were even shadowed as they went about and men kept a careful watch to see that factories were not "window-dressed" for the visit of the official party.

The Inquiry revealed that in 1833 there were relatively few power looms in Bradford. In most of the factories little was carried on but worsted spinning, and it was in this branch of the industry that young children were most employed.

Children who survived infancy, especially girls, were a great asset to their parents, for when husbands were unemployed they became the breadwinners. This was one reason

given by masters for employing young children. Thomas
Holdsworth of Eccleshill said:

> I consider thirteen hours a day, with two hours off for
> meals, not too much for children or adults . . . besides many
> children are the principal support of a family.

Another excuse offered for accepting very young boys and
girls was that parents threatened to take the older ones elsewhere if the young brothers and sisters were not allowed to
start work. In this "joint tyranny" of parents and masters it
is difficult to know who was most to blame. The reply from
the firm of William and Edward Smith said:

> It is the common practice of many parents to bring us
> their younger children at the early age of seven or eight
> years old; but we invariably refuse to listen to them, until
> they actually threaten to take away the other children, and
> then we are frequently compelled against our wills to take
> them about nine years old.

Mr Holdsworth, far from considering the work harmful,
saw it almost as a medicine:

> Frequently, children of a sickly, puny cast, are very much
> improved in health by entering woollen mills, the smell of
> the oil and indigo being very conducive to health; and in
> mills of this description children at eight years old may be
> safely allowed to commence work, as their health will be
> much better by being so employed with a full stomach, than
> letting them run wild in the fields, or in the lanes, with an
> empty one.

In spite of many protests to the contrary, the Commissioners found undoubted instances of children five years
old, who had to work thirteen hours a day, and of nine and
ten year olds who worked fourteen and fifteen hours.

Often during the short meal breaks the machinery had to
be "fettled up" and, at seven in the evening, after a thirteen
hour day, these youngsters had to stay behind and clean the

machines in readiness for morning. Other things which stunted development were malnutrition and lack of sleep and recreation. Few of the children had any home life. They were so tired on Saturday night that they slept all week-end and were just awake in time to begin another round of drudgery by Monday.

Young Richard Turner, reported:

> I was hardly five when I went [to the mill]. I went in petticoats. . . . We used to begin at six, and I have wrought there while seven, eight and nine o'clock at night.

No wonder Parson Bull excused those scholars who couldn't get to his morning Sunday School for eight o'clock.

It was common knowledge that Bradford contained an unusually large number of crippled factory children, whose deformities were caused by continuous stooping, for, as the Inquiry said:

> The old spinning frames of Bradford are built exceedingly low, and this occasions much bending of the knees both in piecening and doffing the bobbins.

The terrors of the factories were the overlookers, who administered cruel punishment for trivial offences, even for talking. Coming late was serious and could result in a fine or a beating.

Many masters were indignant when asked what punishments were used. One said, "We disdain it"; another, "Only a tap or a push"; and another, "No more than in a Sunday School". But boys and girls alike were beaten with straps and ropes, and there was a good deal of striking about the head. In fact, punishment became so much a part of the job that it was expected, and few dare complain for fear that worse might happen to them. Joseph Holmes told the Commissioners:

> I used to get brayed own t'ear at Fawcett's: I can't hear so well w'it. . . . I have another brother that works at mill. He is going eleven. He is crooked. He has been there five

years. He is a piecer. He has been going crooked ever since
he went, I think. . . . There are six children of us altogether
and father has buried three. There are four of us work at
mill: the fifth laiks: he goes to school. He is going six.
Father does not mean him to go to mill.

Undoubtedly there were one or two humane employers
about, but John Wood was an exception. He opened a large
factory school and appointed a doctor to examine the children
weekly; but the majority of the masters either didn't know
what was happening in their own factories or didn't care.

Mr Alfred Power, one of the Commissioners, said:

At Bradford we met with more direct testimony of the
effects of long-continued labour upon the bones of children
in the person of a great number of cripples. . . . We had
reason to believe that we saw but a small proportion of the
cases of deformity existing within the town itself of Bradford.

And his final verdict was:

I can have no hesitation . . . in stating my belief, from
what I saw myself, that a large mass of deformity has been
produced at Bradford by the factory system.

The labour force at Garnett's Barkerend Mills indicates how
much the industry depended on young boys and girls, for out
of 387 hands employed, almost half were under fourteen, and
33 of these were under ten. The day's work began at six and
went on until seven in the evening, but on Saturday, a "half
day", the mill closed at half-past five.

For most workers there was only one meal break, half an
hour for dinner, which enabled those who lived near enough
to hurry home, gulp down the food provided and get back
before the big gates closed. At other times, breakfasts and
"drinkings" were brought to the mill by friends because no
stoppage was allowed.

The treatment of young children in factories at this time
has often been compared with the Slave Trade, and it is

strange that many mill owners who campaigned for an end
to cruelty thousands of miles away saw nothing wrong with
what was happening under their very noses. They permitted
mere infants to work long hours in vile conditions, to be
beaten and crippled, to die prematurely, so that the machines
could be fed and fat profits made.

When the machines were going the people had to be there.
When the threads broke the little pieceners had to get under
the frames and join them together. Men and women were not
in short supply, but there were never enough children to go
round. One employer, when asked if he admitted children
under twelve, said:

> We could not be supplied with a sufficient number of
> children at the age of twelve years and upwards. The pro-
> cess in which the greatest number of young children are
> employed is piecing up the threads in the spinning frame
> as they break. So easy is the labour that it is only fit for a
> young child.

Oastler, Wood, Bull and many other "Ten Hours men"
refused to co-operate with the Commissioners because they
suspected the purpose of the investigation. In a final bid to
enlist the full force of public opinion a huge rally was held at
Low Moor on 1 July 1833, with bands, banners and a platform
of lively speakers. In spite of all their efforts, however, Lord
Ashley's Bill was defeated and an amended version, proposed
by Lord Althorp, was passed.

In some ways the *Althorp Act* of 1833 was a better measure
than the one put forward by Sadler and Lord Ashley. It for-
bade the employment of children under nine and limited the
hours of others to eight a day. The Act also made education
compulsory for two hours each day and provided for the
inspection of factories. But there were too many loopholes,
and those masters who had no intention of keeping the law
found evasion easy. A clause which would have sent them to
a House of Correction after the third offence was omitted from
the new Bill. One of the biggest objections against it was that

children might be made to work in two shifts, perhaps at two different mills—a total of sixteen hours a day. This was possible because the length of the adult working day was uncontrolled.

Whatever the faults of the 1833 Act, it was at least a start. It introduced factory inspection and, in theory at least, made some form of education available to the children. Nevertheless, those who had championed the Ten Hours Bill regarded the *Althorp Act* as a serious blow to their hopes.

After this defeat Oastler campaigned more fiercely than ever, but in 1836 his health broke down and he lost heart. He was then dismissed by his employer, Mr Thornhill, who accused him of embezzlement. Oastler was tried, convicted and placed in the Debtors' Prison, where he remained until his friends paid off the amount he owed. He returned to Huddersfield in triumph and joined in the agitation for reform with renewed vigour, until the death of his wife. After this sad blow he retired and went to live in London.

The Ten Hours Movement was gaining ground, however, and an Act of 1844, although it lowered the age of employment to eight, reduced the working day for those under thirteen to six-and-a-half hours and made half-time education compulsory. Oastler, still not content, came north once again to conduct a tour in support of a new Bill limiting working hours for women and young people under eighteen to ten hours a day, an Act which became law in 1847. To mark this success the partners Wood and Walker entertained three thousand workpeople to a substantial meal in the grounds of Bolling Hall.

Fourteen years later Richard Oastler died on his way to Harrogate, and his funeral took place at Kirkstall, where members of the Short Time Committee carried him to the grave which already held his wife and two children. Bradford was selected as the site for a national memorial and Oastler's statue was placed just outside the old Midland Station.

While great efforts were being made to improve the lot of the factory children, another set of young workers were in an even worse plight. In coal mines around Bradford, boys and girls from five and upwards worked as trappers and hurriers. It is true that in Bradford girls were not usually employed, but in evidence to the Children's Employment Commission of 1842 Thomas Mackley, a surgeon, said that in Wilsden, four miles from the town, at least nine girls were working in mines. He described their occupation:

> They have a chain or belt about the waist, which passes between the legs of the female, and is hooked on to the waggon of coals [the corves], which they pull from the place where the men work to the bottom of the shaft. I should also add, that the men in the pit work perfectly naked.

The Report speaks of these children as being

> Chained, belted, harnessed, like dogs in a go-cart—black, saturated with wet, and more than half naked—crawling upon their hands and feet, and dragging their heavy loads behind them.

Sometimes the corves were pushed along the rails, with head and outstretched arms, the process of moving the coals to the shaft being known as "hurrying".

Children in the most pathetic case were the "trappers", who, the Report says, sat in a little hole scooped out for them in the side of the gates behind each door. There they sat, string in hand, ready to open the door the moment they heard a corve approaching. When the corve had passed through they allowed the door to close by its own weight. Apart from freeing the door if it stuck, this is all they had to do, for twelve hours, day in day out. They were allowed no light, but spent their lives "in solitude, damp and darkness". This was the biggest grievance—the darkness. One boy of nine said, "I never see the daylight except on Sundays".

Children went into the pits regularly at the age of five; many at seven, but most at eight. One collier at Birkenshaw, on the outskirts of Bradford, was known to have taken his own child to "hurry" at three, but this, mercifully, was an exception. When the child was exhausted he was carried home, stripped and put to bed.

Many of the employers admitted they knew nothing—literally nothing—about the children in their own mines. They were not aware either of the time they began work, or the time they finished, and as to meals and general welfare they were "profoundly ignorant".

The owners paid the colliers and left it to them to recruit their own labour as they wished. Very often a father took his own children, boys or girls, as soon as they were able to push a corve or open a trap door. The hours of employment were not strictly regulated, and night work, even for children, was part of the system in mines owned by the iron companies. There the furnaces burnt continuously, and on Sundays work was non-stop from 6 a.m., for twenty-four hours, shifts operating on alternate week-ends.

The Low Moor Company and Bowling Iron Works, where conditions were rather better than in most mines, professed not to employ girls at all. At the former, however, two girls were found to be working above ground, helping their fathers. One of them, Ellen Barraclough, aged twelve, had been there for four years, and seemed happy enough in her own way. The day began at six, but the girl said she could not go to Sunday School because on that day she worked in the morning, from four until nine. Mary Patchett, aged fourteen, was employed about the furnace, carrying coals. She didn't like the work, but said it wasn't more than she could manage.

On the whole the children were apallingly ignorant, few being able to read or write at all. One little boy didn't know his age, or even what a birthday was; he said he hadn't got one.

Samuel Scriven, one of the Commissioners, went underground to see what conditions were like for himself. In a dress of "flannel, clogs and knee caps" he bravely surmounted the dangers, sometimes creeping on hands and knees, and in one place, where the passage was very low, crawling, as he said, "like a turtle". Once he rode on a corve, with head hanging over the back and legs over the front, "in anticipation of getting scalped". Accidents were, indeed, frequent occurrences, and human life was so cheap that even fatal accidents were not bound to be reported before 1850.

The owners showed little concern about what children did in their few leisure hours, although the Low Moor Company built a day school for general use in 1814—Scott's School. In spite of this the Rev. Joshua Fawcett, the Curate of Low Moor Church, told the Commission that, in his opinion, four-fifths of the young population received no education whatever.

Home life contained few pleasures and little refinement. Mr Fawcett said he knew a house where a family of fourteen slept in one room, and others where all the children of whatever age, sometimes as many as ten, shared the same bedroom. Factory Acts improved working conditions and removed many injustices, but in the face of such widespread ignorance, education was the only remedy.

By good chance W. E. Forster came to Bradford in the very year the Commission was gathering evidence, and it became his ambition to give every child the right to a sound, regular education.

John James regarded it as almost inevitable that, among factory workers, all but a favoured few would have to tread "rugged and unhealthy paths" and eat the bread of hard labour all the days of their lives. The masters lived, if not like princes, in considerable comfort in big houses, while their workpeople were crammed into insanitary hovels. General discontent caused by low wages, or no wages at all, and bad conditions, was shown in strikes and riots—the only effective means of protest open to the working classes. In 1837 Bradford was the scene of ugly riots caused by the introduction of the new Poor Law, which had been passed three years earlier.

Before this date poor relief had been the responsibility of each individual township or parish, with the result that a very heavy burden was placed on the ratepayers in some areas.

H

Reform was badly needed on many counts, and the Poor Law Amendment Act of 1834 was an attempt to organize relief on a national basis. For this purpose parishes were united, the Bradford Union consisting of the whole parish, except Haworth, with the addition of outer townships, such as Tong, Idle and Pudsey. In Bradford thirty-two Guardians were appointed to administer the scheme.

The general policy was to give relief only to those who entered workhouses, which were so like prisons they were known as "Bastilles". Here the object was to make life so unpleasant that men would gladly accept the lowest wages to get out, and a man separated from wife and family was under intolerable pressure to do so.

To help the Guardians, the Government appointed Assistant Commissioners, and very tactlessly sent Mr Alfred Power, an old "enemy of the people", to meet the Bradford Board at the Court House. Bull, Oastler and others were quick to draw attention to the scandal which allowed men like Mr Power, a Factory Commissioner, to do two jobs and draw salaries amounting to £2,000 a year.

On Monday 30 October 1837 unruly mobs disturbed the meeting at the Court House and it was transferred to the Sun Inn. Later in the day, however, the Guardians returned to the Court House and the public were admitted. When the meeting was over, a crowd gathered and pelted Mr Power with mud and stones as he returned to his rooms at the Sun Inn.

Another meeting arranged for a fortnight later was adjourned because of possible violence, after which Mr Power asked for military aid. When he arrived for the meeting, on 20 November, forty Hussars were stationed in the town. The meeting took place in the Court House behind barricaded doors, and outside crowds grew until midday, when five or six thousand people were trying to get in. There was some stone throwing, and after the Riot Act had been read, the soldiers were ordered to clear the Court House yard and steps. After this, a few of the rioters made their way to the back of the building and began to smash windows.

Peace was restored, but when the Guardians left the meeting they were followed and had to seek shelter in a warehouse to escape from volleys of stones. In the afternoon the soldiers retired, upon which crowds again assembled at the Court House and smashed almost every pane of glass. When the Hussars returned they met with strong resistance, but as evening drew on the soldiers, losing patience, used their pistols and "the edge of the sword" to disperse the mob. As a result of the disorders several people were taken for trial to York Castle. It was to deal with disturbances such as this that Bradford Moor Barracks was built in 1844.

Poor Law riots were followed in 1840 by Chartist riots, Chartism being a movement in support of a "People's Charter", which contained six points, including manhood suffrage—votes even for working men—secret ballots and annual Parliaments. Some of the Chartists were prepared to take up arms to achieve their ends, and in Bradford the leader of the rebels was "Fat" Peter Bussey, an ex-woolcomber who was then landlord of the Roebuck Inn. An ambitious and rather ridiculous plan had been formed, which included siezing arms and ammunition from the Low Moor Ironworks and marching with them to London, presumably as part of a larger plot. At two o'clock on the morning of 27 January 1840 a number of armed men appeared in the Green Market, expecting to find thousands more. They captured two watchmen, but the rocket signal which should have brought in big battalions did not go off. In the end sixteen of the rebels were taken and sentenced at York Castle to periods of imprisonment. Chartist agitation went on for another ten years in Bradford and eventually, of course, the main points in the "People's Charter" were granted.

The plug-drawing riots were simpler, but more effective demonstrations. The aim of the plug-drawers was to remove plugs from boilers and rake out the fires so that the engines could not run. Disturbances took place in Lancashire and Yorkshire, and Sunday 14 August 1842 was the scene of a big rally at Bradford Moor. The next day a march towards

Halifax began at the Oddfellows' Hall. On the way the demonstrators called out workpeople from the factories, and the increasing crowds played havoc in the engine rooms, putting many of them out of action. This form of Luddism did not last very long, but it was the cause of much expense and inconvenience to mill owners.

At about this time the *Leeds Mercury* sounded a warning that the need for manual labour might soon be overcome by the "general and sudden introduction of machines". This prophecy did not come true at once, but the prodigious output of yarn from steam driven mills made the advent of power looms inevitable. Then, all that remained was to get rid of the antiquated method of combing wool by hand, a reform desirable but difficult to achieve.

A factor which slowed up but did not prevent the use of power looms was the low level of weavers' wages. One report, for instance, gave details of weavers who only took home 7s 7½d a week. With such cheap labour available it is not surprising that masters were in no hurry to invest in machines which might come under "Enoch's hammer". So, for a while after the 1825 strike, handloom weavers had little competition in Bradford. By 1838 the industry was in a state of transition, hand looms and power looms often being found side by side in the same factory; but once the advantages were seen, power looms took over, hand-weavers being either sacked or laid off. Weaving, formerly a man's job, could now be done by women and girls, who often "minded" a pair of looms.

There was not much choice of work for the unemployed. Some trained as overlookers or "tacklers", the highly skilled mechanics of the day. Some turned to hand-combing, an already overcrowded, badly paid job; while strong young men went into the pits or quarries. Unemployment among hand-weavers in all parts of the country increased so much that it became a national problem and emigration was encouraged.

9. EXPANDING TRADE AND THE
RAILWAYS

In the 1830s Bradford was "invaded" by a small band of merchants, many of them Germans, from Leeds. They did not take over the town, but they exerted a powerful influence on trade and on the affairs of Bradford generally. The *Yorkshire Observer* of 1836 reported:

> The Manufacturers are removing to Bradford as fast as they can get accommodated with rooms; and so long as the merchants can get what they want at the latter place, it is not likely they will attend Halifax.

The Bradford Piece Hall had become a very popular place, in contrast with the halls at Halifax, Wakefield and Leeds, which were being deserted by the manufacturers and merchants. The change was so great that Robert Baker, writing about the industrial economy of Leeds, said:

> A few years ago, there were in Leeds many Stuff merchants carrying on a large business, buying goods principally at Bradford and selling them at Leeds. But on a sudden panic, during which they supposed that Bradford was about to absorb the whole Stuff Trade, and that their customers would never be seen in Leeds at all, they fled thither . . . leaving the manufacturers only behind them, who would have flown too, but for their mills, which they could neither carry away nor dispose of.

Merchants were a very powerful force, for although they made no contribution to the manufacturing process themselves, they were at the "money end" of the trade, where transactions were concluded and bills paid. They simplified the business of selling and introduced manufactured goods to new customers and wider markets. Because they both bought pieces and arranged the dyeing and finishing to their customers' requirements, they were able, in many ways, to dictate fashion and "call the tune".

Bradford's worsteds were in great demand but the town was so badly off for dyehouses that when George Ripley moved from Halifax to set up his vats in a cottage in Milligan's Lane, Bowling, he had only three competitors. Thirty years later their numbers had hardly increased; and so long as dyeing remained a "Cinderella" industry Bradford was bound to be a mere workshop for towns which were better equipped in this branch of the trade.

Largely through the initiative of Edward Ripley and Sons, who were the pioneers in black dyeing—a strangely popular shade with the working classes—and in the method of dealing with pieces made from wool and cotton, Bradford gradually gained a wide reputation as a dyeing centre. The Bradford Dyers' Association, known simply as the BDA, became the largest combine of its kind in the world. Figures indicate the extent of the change. In 1822 Bradford had 5 worsted merchants and Leeds 24, but by 1861 Leeds had only 17 and Bradford 157, over a third of whom were foreigners, mostly Germans.

The first of these "settlers" was Leo Schuster, who bought a plot of land near Market Street for a warehouse in 1836. Jacob Behrens, a distinguished name in Bradford's history, came to Leeds in 1832 but moved to Bradford six years later to be "on the spot". This marks the beginning of the great era of warehouse building in the Packover area, which earned it the name of "Little Germany".

These immigrants—Schuster, Behrens, Kessler, Zossenheim, Semon and Moser, to name only a few—played a vital part in extending trade, and many of them became civic leaders with great records of public service. Julius Delius, a German who set up business as a wool merchant in Bradford in 1850, was on the committee which arranged concerts for the Halle Orchestra. Julius became a wealthy man, bringing up his family of fourteen children in comparative luxury; but it was his son Frederick who made the name Delius famous. Fortunately for music he turned his back on wool, left Bradford, and went off to grow oranges in Florida.

The efforts of this growing band of influential merchants, particularly those with connections across the North Sea, put a great strain on the turnpike road to Leeds along which, by 1830, heavy loads of undyed pieces were being despatched from Bradford. This traffic emphasized the need for a rail connection with Leeds, which, in turn, helped to put the Bradford Canal out of business.

It seems like heresy to suggest that the expansion of the worsted industry was due, even in part, to the use of cotton : yet it is true. Power loom weaving placed a great strain on the warp threads, and cotton, being stronger and cheaper than wool, was found to be an excellent substitute.

James Parker, in his book *Hipperholme to Tong*, called the introduction of cotton warps "a revolution", and attributed the rapid rise of both the town and its trade to their use. After 1834 most worsted goods were woven with cotton warps, a combination which produced completely new types of cloth in astounding varieties. This, of course, brought complaints that things weren't what they used to be; as one local poet put it :

> *Before these sad, degenerate days,*
> *The time is not forgotten*
> *When Bradford piece goods were all stuff*
> *And were not warped with cotton.*

The old hands felt that the trade was "going to the dogs", but cotton warps increased the scope of manufacturers and speeded up mechanization. They also added to Bradford's problems by throwing more hand-loom weavers out of work.

Now that power looms were being perfected, only wool-combing remained in its primitive state. Cartwright had invented a mechanical comb in 1785, but the "Big Bens" were not a success. They were tried out by Robert Ramsbotham and others, but after fifty years, in spite of costly experiments, most wool was still combed by hand. In the end it was the initiative and genius of Samuel Lister which provided the worsted industry with an effective means of mechanical combing.

At the age of seventeen, while Samuel Marsden was rearing sheep at Botany Bay, Samuel Cunliffe Lister of Bradford was selling shawls in America. It was because he was "too young to do anything else" that the future Lord Masham had been appointed as commercial traveller to his brother John, who managed the mill at Shipley Fields built by their father.

Ellis Cunliffe took the additional name of Lister when he inherited the Manningham estates, through his wife, and went to live at Manningham Hall in 1809. Among his possessions was the Spotted House, formerly the Lister's Arms, and it was here that he held court as magistrate. "Justice Lister" gained a reputation for fair dealing and he was an obvious choice as Member for Bradford when the Reform Act of 1832 gave the town its first two MPs. The other Member was John Hardy, one of the founders of the Low Moor Company, who lived at the Manor Hall.

After building Red Beck Mills at Shipley in 1815 Mr Lister erected two others in quick succession, Miry Pond, at Great Horton, and Mitchell Bros' Mill in Bowling Old Lane. These were followed twenty years later by Manningham Mills, which was opened by his sons under the name of J. and S. C. Lister, in 1838. Samuel Lister had acted as clerk of works during the building, superintending operations both on the site and at Lister's own Daisy Hill Quarry, from which the stone was taken. Manningham Old Mill, as it was called, had barely opened before it was almost blown down during a terrific gale.

John Lister, having "come into money", left the family business, and Samuel gave up manufacturing to concentrate on woolcombing. Although he had spent much of his time travelling, especially to America, "Sam" knew enough about machinery by 1844 to patent a device for fringing shawls. Henceforward he was for ever risking his money on apparently hopeless ventures.

His first big gamble was to pay £12,000 for Donisthorpe's combing machine in order to improve it. He took Donisthorpe into partnership and in 1843, with James Ambler's help, produced the very first sample of fine, machine combed botany. Lord Masham, in his later years, was not altogether modest about this achievement. He said :

"It had taken me just three years to do what the whole trade and a host of inventors had failed to do in fifty, and what looked to be at the time almost impossible."

Lister soon had orders for fifty machines from two Bradford firms alone, and by devoting the entire resources of Manningham Mills to woolcombing found himself, in 1855 at the age

S. C. Lister

of forty, a very rich man. He was at the head of a business, with branches in this country and on the Continent, "such as the world had never known". In the previous year he got married and "did nothing", but in 1855 he took out twelve patents—one a month.

The future of woolcombing now seemed assured. Samuel Marsden's botany and Samuel Lister's machine comb had helped to place Bradford in the forefront of the worsted industry, but it was at the expense of the hands who, in 1844, hissed the inventor as he stood on the balcony of the old Town Hall.

Unfortunately much bitterness and many law suits arose between those who claimed credit for the improvements. Lister acknowledged Cartwright and no other as his master, but the name of Sir Isaac Holden, who worked with Lister for ten years, will always be remembered. James Noble's circular comb set the final seal on the efforts of all who had striven, from Cartwright onwards.

The new machines had an immediate effect on trade. The price of worsted yarns decreased, the whole manufacturing process was speeded up, and in a very short time thousands of hand-combers were thrown out of work. Some men found jobs on the machines, but many more had either to seek other employment or move, with their families, out of the Bradford district. Redundancy on such a scale made the woolcombers' plight desperate indeed.

The Woolcombers' Aid Association was formed and attempts were made to find jobs in other parts of the country. One advertisement ran:

Wanted: Situations as Passenger or Goods Porters for 100 Strong, Active, Honest and Industrious Woolcombers from 22 to 40 years of age, varying in height from 5ft 6in to 6ft.

And where all else failed a man might, like Thomas Cavanagh, try to emigrate, begging his fare by means of a testimonial:

The Bearer of this, Thomas Cavanagh, belongs to that unfortunate class of Operatives, the Woolcombers. . . . He has been out of work since 11 March last and has in vain sought employment since that date. He has tried to acquire the trade of painter, but has failed through the slackness which pervades that branch of business. His only resource is *Emigration*. . . . A small donation from twenty or thirty persons would thus, in all human probability rescue a young man from the jaws of Pauperism.

The help given by the Woolcombers' Aid Association was very much appreciated. George Hopton, who wrote to the Secretary thanking him, liked his new job in Middlesborough and wanted to make a home there. He said :

as sone as i see a chance i in tend to take one and have my famley heare for i think i Could do veary well if i had them heare for i like the place veary well . . . and i have got veary deesent lodgins.

Poor wages and the laborious nature of the work caused many exiles to return home. Hopton stuck it out, although he complained :

At sume lodgines hear thay will not heaven mend your stocking for you and thay charge half a Crowne a week.

The story of the displacement of these semi-skilled, illiterate men makes sorry reading. By 1845 a crisis had been reached and a committee was appointed to enquire into the condition of the working classes in Bradford. Three years later £2,000 was allocated from the rates to help those who wished to leave the country. Within ten years neither handloom weavers nor hand-combers were required : the worsted industry had at last become fully mechanized.

Mechanization elsewhere was rapidly increasing, particularly in transport. The Stockton-on-Tees to Darlington

Railway was completed in 1825, and when the Leeds to Selby
line had been constructed attempts were made to put Bradford on the railway map as quickly as possible. In fact, during
sixteen frustrating years no fewer than fourteen proposals
were submitted to Parliament. Bradford's natural disadvantages—someone said the town was "built in a hole"—made
any through line a particularly awkward and costly piece of
engineering. Nevertheless, five of the proposed schemes
contained plans for crossing the town by means of
viaducts.

By 1830 the wear and tear on the Bradford-Leeds turnpike
road, caused mainly by the piece goods trade, was so great
that it was impossible to keep the surface in repair. The need
to open up a speedy route for Bradford goods to the Continent,
a trade in which Leeds merchants played a big part, was the
main reason for the drive to connect the two towns by rail.
One argument against the introduction of railways was that
they would put the canals out of action, which of course they
did; but before any railway was made in Bradford, business
men preferred the short, direct way to Leeds, rather than the
circuitous canal route.

The proposal, in 1830, to link Bradford with the Selby line,
brought in subscriptions amounting to £200,000, much of
of which was lost when the scheme was abandoned. The
intention was to build a station in the region of Hammerton
Street, and take the line through Laisterdyke to Stanningley,
and thence to Wortley, near Leeds. But the engineer's
estimates increased as time went on, and land owners lodged
serious objections to the scheme. In the end, the proposers
themselves presented a petition against the Bill as it was going
through Parliament, and the project was dropped. For the
time being Bradford had to content itself with a connection
made by horse-drawn omnibuses at Brighouse station—*Brighouse for Bradford*, as it was called.

In planning a railway from Bradford to Leeds there were
two main choices of route: the first, direct, via Stanningley,
and the second on a line following the Bradford Canal, with

an eastward turn at Shipley, to go along the Aire Valley. In the maze of proposals subsequently put forward there was great rivalry between the "Short Liners" and those, like George Stephenson, who preferred the roundabout route.

In 1843 some Bradford men with shares in the North Midland Company approached their chairman, George Hudson— the "Railway King"—with a request for a line to the town. The matter was discussed and a decision taken to construct a Leeds–Bradford railway. The engineer was to be Robert Stephenson, and the route he chose was the Valley line, which his father had recommended five years earlier.

Although the length was said to be 13½ miles as against 9 or 10, there was not much difference in the estimated costs of the respective lines, and it was thought that the level, roundabout route would be cheaper to operate. One difficulty about the short line was a "most severe gradient" at Laisterdyke, but the other route was not without its hazards. The Aire had to be crossed six times, and the Leeds–Liverpool Canal four; besides which a long tunnel had to be made at Thackley and a viaduct with ten arches at Apperley.

In its passage through Parliament the Leeds and Bradford Railway Bill was opposed by the Manchester and Leeds Board, who were themselves planning a link with Bradford. The Bill was passed, however, and received the Royal Assent on 4 July 1844. Because of the strong opposition the Act was approved on a promise "to connect at Bradford with a line through Halifax to the Manchester and Leeds Railway at Sowerby Bridge." Unfortunately, to keep the promise meant crossing the centre of Bradford, a thing no railway has ever been able to do.

Work began in earnest and, in spite of all difficulties the "contractor's opening" of the Leeds–Bradford line took place on 30 May 1846, according to the *Bradford Observer*, "one of the most glorious days that ever shone". The "Lindsay" left Leeds for Bradford, pulling a train with five hundred people aboard, a plentiful supply of flags, champagne, cigars, and two bands of music. The guests were startled at Kirkstall Forge by a burst of artillery fire—a welcome volley from a few small cannon—and were greeted at Armley with vociferous cheers from "the hearty natives". The journey included a ten minute stop at Shipley, to water the iron steed, and at two o'clock, an hour after starting, the train reached Bradford.

On the return journey the train stopped for a while on the Apperley Viaduct: at Kirkstall there was more cannon fire, and passengers were amused to see that some of the spectators below were carrying banners saying, "No Bastilles" and "Free Trade". At Leeds the contractor's party adjourned to the White Horse for a magnificent meal.

After sixteen years of waiting Bradford was at last linked with the national system and 30 June, the date of the official opening, was observed as a general holiday. At ten o'clock that morning a hundred and fifty guests assembled at the Bradford end, ready, and in good time it must be said, to depart at eleven. At eleven o'clock the train had not arrived, and at half-past there was still no train. The English summer weather broke in torrents of rain, and the railway, living up to a reputation it had not yet gained, got a train to Kirkgate three-quarters of an hour late. Meanwhile, the passengers had admired the lavish luncheon prepared for them in the specially erected pavilion: colossal amounts of food, including 20 lambs, 54 ducks and 60 chickens.

The train at last set off, but at Shipley Junction the guests were staggered to see the directors' train, and another from Leeds, approach and pass them. When the Bradford party reached Leeds the station was deserted and there was not so much as a biscuit to be had. After kicking their heels for three-quarters of an hour the Bradfordians returned, as the report said, "whence they came"; unfortunately too late to do anything more than eat up the remnants left by their Leeds rivals. They no doubt made up for it in the evening, when over a thousand guests sat down to a magnificent dinner.

On the following day, 1 July, the Leeds–Bradford line opened for passengers, with an hourly, non-stop service, but it was non-stop simply because there were as yet no intermediate stations. The *Bradford Observer* concludes its light-hearted account of these memorable events with the remark that the passengers grumbled because the fare was too high. From now on, journeys to London and day trips to the seaside were available to all.

Twenty years later, on 16 November 1866, the service was interrupted in a most spectacular manner. Several days of torrential rain were followed by a furious storm, during which the 4.50 passenger train to Leeds crossed the Apperley Viaduct. Some of the passengers who alighted at Rawdon told the station master that they were certain they felt the track move, a fear confirmed by the crew. A freight train which followed came to a halt over the third arch as masonry fell into the river. The line was steadily sinking. The crew ran off in both directions to give warning of the danger, and after about quarter of an hour the train plunged into the torrent below. Fortunately there was no loss of life and the bridge was quickly repaired.

In an effort to keep its promise the Leeds and Bradford Board obtained permission to build a junction line from Manningham, about a mile from the town, to join the West Riding Union line in Well Street. This was to be done by means of two arches over Broadstones, near the Parish Church, and a diversion of Canal Road. A model of the proposed plan was prepared, but there the scheme ended.

The development of railways around Bradford after 1846 forms a most complicated study: suffice to say here that the town was gradually encircled by small stations, each with its own station master and booking hall, while close by there was often a coal depot and goods yard. Even after the introduction of tramcars it was quite usual to travel to Bradford by train, from places like Manningham and Laisterdyke—a penny or twopenny ride.

Eventually, three main companies dominated the field: the Midland, operating from Kirkgate; the Lancashire and York-shire with its depot in Drake Street, near the site of the Exchange Station, and the Great Northern, which catered for

The Apperley Viaduct Disaster

both goods and passengers at Adolphus Street. In 1867 this last became a goods station only and the passenger traffic was transferred to the Exchange, where a new station was built twenty years later. A feature of this station was that the ten platforms, under the two large arches, were shared by the Lancashire and Yorkshire and the Great Northern companies. Near the centre of the town, at Bridge Street and Valley Road, and a little further afield at City Road, there were goods depots with large storage warehouses for wool.

In 1897 an Act was passed authorizing the Midland Company to extend its line from Royston, south-east of Wakefield, to Bradford. In this plan the railway was to follow an almost straight course through Oakenshaw to Manningham, crossing the centre of Bradford by means of a tunnel. Property along the route was purchased, contracts were allocated, and a start was made in 1902. Four years later the scheme was abandoned as impracticable. At this point the *Bradford Observer* commented :

> Bradford is to-day "on a siding" and there, if this scheme is allowed to lapse, it may remain till the crack of doom.

Nothing daunted, a further attempt was made and in 1911 a Bill was passed embodying proposals to span the centre of the town by a viaduct just east of the Exchange Station. This ambitious scheme, with provision for a two-decker station, one level for use as a terminus and the other as a through line, never got beyond the blue-print stage. Finally, the declaration of war in 1914 dashed all hopes of progress.

In the end, Bradford was left with two main stations separated by an unbridgeable gap of three hundred yards. The Midland, on the north side, was at ground level: the Exchange, on the south side was thirty feet up.

The only through line Bradford had, or is likely to have, is the one shown on Dixon's map of 1844, which hopefully shows a railway linking the proposed station of the West Riding Union (Exchange) and the Kirkgate (Midland) station.

The Great Exhibition of 1851, held under the glass roof of a huge pavilion in Hyde Park, gave a great stimulus to British trade, not least to the worsted industry, with its new found combing power.

Before the introduction of railways a visit to London for most workers would have been a mere dream, but now it came within the bounds of possibility. The railway companies were out to capture business and agreed upon a return fare of 16s 2d during the Exhibition. The arrangement fell through, however, and cut-throat competition between the Great Northern and Midland lines brought the price down to just over five shillings. Advertising took a simpler form then, and the tidings were made known in the streets of Bradford by means of a brass band, at the head of which—drum-major-like—marched a man carrying a placard announcing the reductions.

Bradford took the Exhibition to its heart, contributing more money to the central fund than any other town of similar size.

Unlike Leeds, whose display was said to be "more like a woollen draper's shop", Bradford showed off its goods in splendid style, behind 1,500 feet of solid plate glass, an effort which was rewarded by twelve medals for cloth and nine for yarns. Donisthorpe's combing machine also received a Council Medal, and wool was so much to the fore that the only other exhibits from Bradford were said to be a hand painted table and a pair of artificial legs.

Success at the Exhibition was a good start to the second half of the nineteenth century in Bradford, but there was cause for concern among manufacturers. The French enjoyed a marked superiority in the production of all wool cloths, Bradford having gone in for quantity rather than quality, and the design of Bradford's fancy goods left much to be desired. In the end the ill wind blew some good, because it was a wish to improve designing skills that led to the opening of the Technical College in 1882.

When the Great Exhibition was over, the building in Hyde Park was offered for sale. Titus Salt went to London, with Mr Lockwood, the architect, to see whether part of it could be transported to Saltaire for use as a weaving shed. Because the structure was not thought to be substantial enough the plan was abandoned, and the hope of a permanent souvenir was lost.

10. THE BRADFORD CHARTER

The year 1847 marks Bradford's coming of age, for until then, although the population had risen to something like 80,000, the town was still being governed on "parish pump" principles. It grew up in disorder, without adequate drainage or water supply, but there was never any shortage of drink of another kind—gin, and the good Yorkshire ale Defoe found so much to his liking. As a consequence, by 1831, when a police force was thought necessary, crime was high and moral standards were very low.

A surgeon reporting to the *Factories Inquiry Commission* of 1833, said:

> I look upon Bradford as a very ill-regulated town in every respect; badly drained, wretchedly cleaned, until very recently. . . . We had the cholera in one district chiefly, called Wapping. I think we had more than one hundred cases and between thirty and forty deaths. In this neighbourhood there is a great deal of loom-weaving. They sleep and work in the same room frequently.

And in 1845 James Smith, in a *Report on the Sanitary Condition of Bradford*, laid the blame fairly and squarely on the fact that the main sewers were discharged into the beck and the canal basin. He said:

> The water of this basin is so often charged with decaying matter, that in hot weather bubbles of sulphuretted hydrogen are continually rising to the surface, and so much is the atmosphere loaded with that gas, that watch-cases and other materials of silver become black in the pockets of the work-

men employed near the canal. The stench is sometimes very strong and fevers prevail much all around. Taking the general condition of Bradford, I am obliged to pronounce it to be the most filthy town I have visited.

Two years later the *Bradford Observer*, speaking of the disease and unemployment in the town, said that the condition of hundreds of families was "sufficient to drive even wise men to madness and desperation". The state of muddle is not surprising, however, for the two Boards which governed the town, the Lighting and Watching Commissioners, and the Surveyors, had not much power. To make matters worse, they met in private, levied separate rates and, altogether, were not on very good terms.

The townships of Bowling, Manningham, Horton and Bradford were such close neighbours that whatever one did affected the others, and it was obvious that for the common good they ought to combine forces. In 1843, the Lighting and Watching Commissioners, aware of the need to improve conditions, were about to apply for increased powers, but the *Bradford Observer* advised them to ask for a Mayor and Town Council, as Sheffield had done. With this in mind a public meeting of ratepayers was called, at which it was decided to make application to the Privy Council for a Charter of Incorporation.

This decision angered some of the Commissioners and Surveyors, who wished to retain their authority, and their opposition was so strong that a Government inquiry was held to consider the whole question. When a vote was taken the objectors had a majority of two thousand, but those in favour of a Charter campaigned vigorously and the decision later went in their favour. Accordingly, in April 1847, the young Queen Victoria signed the Charter putting Bradford "under new management", with permission to elect a mayor, fourteen aldermen and forty-two councillors. Henceforward the inhabitants of the new borough were to be "for ever one body politic and corporate in deed, fact and name."

The first Mayor was Robert Milligan, a Scotsman. He was a partner in the important firm of Milligan, Forbes and Company, whose fine merchant warehouse stood next to the Court House in Hall Ings. The Court House has gone, but Milligan's warehouse is now the headquarters of the Bradford and District Newspaper Company, where the *Telegraph and Argus* is printed.

Having been granted Borough status Bradford was awarded a coat of arms which was already familiar, the emblems of the boar legend. It is perhaps unfortunate that the town's dependence on wool is not commemorated, but a suggestion of Bradford's trade came with the addition of Supporters in 1907 —a "Ram Sable" and an "Angola Goat Argent".

Angola is another form of the word *Angora*, Ankara, the capital of Turkey, where the angora goat was originally bred. And while mohair is not by any means the same thing as botany wool, the choice of the "Angola Goat", from which mohair comes, reminds us that large consignments of hairs— especially mohair and alpaca—were processed by Bradford firms and went into Bradford cloths. There was some regret, nevertheless, that wool was not commemorated on the coat of arms, and there were some wry remarks about the other Supporter, the "Ram Sable", which was referred to as the "black sheep". The Cathedral made amends, when it chose its crest, by placing a woolsack on its shield, above St Peter's Keys.

The symbols on the Bradford Arms tell their own story; the three horns stand for the three calls John Northrop gave to welcome the lord of the manor, while the sprouting tree above the boar's head represents Cliffe Wood, and the well the drinking place there. The boar is always without tongue.

There were differences about the choice of a Motto, and the Latin tag "Labor Omnia Vincit" was not to everybody's liking. One councillor is said to have expressed a preference for " 'es nowt; is nowt", which being interpreted means, "Those who *have* nothing *are* nothing". In view of the slavery in Bradford's mills it certainly seemed unnecessary to stress the virtue of hard work.

The most pressing problem facing the new council was how to accommodate the ever increasing population, which rose, during the first half of the nineteenth century, from 13,264 to 103,771. The influx of Irish immigrants, mainly due to the potato famine of 1845–6, placed an added strain on the town's feeble resources. It is estimated that twenty per cent of the inhabitants of the four townships were outsiders, and that half of these were Irish families, usually housed in the poorest quarters of the town.

The Irish came ready and willing to work, but did not receive a very warm welcome from Bradford's large army of unemployed. Efforts were made to persuade them to leave Bradford, and the Board of Guardians, who were administering the new Poor Law, made a decision in 1847 that "all Irish and Scotch applicants for relief be passed home". Besides, most of the Irish were Roman Catholics, and the reappearance of the old faith aroused considerable alarm and controversy in the town.

In the face of many threats this persevering minority, after worshipping in the Roebuck Inn, showed their determination by celebrating High Mass at Stott Hill, under the very shadow of the Parish Church. St Mary's Chapel was consecrated in 1825, but the next church, St Patrick's, did not open until 1853. After this there was a steady succession of churches—St Peter's, St Ann's and St Joseph's—and St Mary's Chapel was eventually replaced, in 1876, by the fine church in East Parade.

The fact that there was no form of transport available to ordinary people compelled them to live near their places of work. Houses, mainly back-to-backs, with communal privies, sometimes in the ratio of forty people to one convenience, were being erected near mills. Twice the council tried to ban the building of back-to-backs, but more and more houses had to be provided. Squalid and insanitary as they were, back-to-backs proved more attractive than basement kitchens or lodging houses.

Goit Side, near the corn mill, was an area where there was

a particularly heavy concentration of Irish immigrants. In Thompson's Buildings, near Thompson's Mill, one of Bradford's first factories, a survey of 1861 showed that on an average eight people occupied one room, and four slept in each bed. The newcomers had roofs over their heads, it is true, but overcrowding was on a scandalously high scale. Those who lived in basement kitchens alongside the goit fared worst of all. When the channel overflowed epidemics broke out, and diseases we now think little of, such as scarlet fever, were dreaded.

A drive on hygiene and health education was a crying need, as the Baths and Cemetery Committee found in 1868 when it regretted to observe "the excessive death rate which continues to prevail among children under five". Things had not improved much by 1876, when over two thousand infants died, half of them before they were a year old. Yet the town's health inspectors waged a ceaseless campaign against dirt and disease. In eight years £100,000 had been spent on sewers, and the systematic removal of refuse was a great step forward.

Bradford was a place where the supply of water could never keep pace with demand. The town's first pipeline ran from Haycliffe Hill to a field behind the Old House at Home and from there to a reservoir in Westgate. The residents of the small central area round about the Manor Hall, the only ones supplied from this source, drew their water from standpipes.

The council quickly took over the responsibilities of the private Waterworks Company, but in 1858 supplies ran out and the townspeople were reduced either to using wells or buying water from barrels. After more local reservoirs had been constructed an ambitious scheme for bringing water from the upper reaches of the Nidd, forty miles away, was sanctioned.

This undertaking required the construction of three great lakes in the valley below Little Whernside. The largest of these reservoirs, Scar House, which did not come into use until about 1936, was built behind a massive dam thought to be the highest in Europe.

On 14 July 1904, one of the great days in the history of Bradford Waterworks, a large body of officials went by special train to watch the Mayor cut the first sod on the line of the Nidd Valley Light Railway. Higher up the valley, at Angram, Alderman Holdsworth turned the first spadeful of soil on the embankment of the new reservoir. Permission to construct the railway, a standard gauge line, was granted to the Corporation on condition that the first six miles, from Pateley Bridge to Lofthouse, should be open to passengers. The line remained in operation until the completion of Scar House, but the last passengers were carried in 1929.

After 1847 a sense of civic pride gave rise to concern about some of the buildings in the town centre, and the deplorable condition of the Manor Hall, once one of Bradford's most dignified residences, compelled the Corporation to take action.

William Rawson, lord of the manor, replaced the old Bradford Hall by a new building in 1705, and for a hundred years the family lived there in a style befitting their station. One eye-witness, for example, told how the two Misses Rawson added a little colour to Sunday observance by walking down Kirkgate to the Parish Church preceded by a jester, in cap and bells, carrying their prayer books on a cushion.

The next tenant was John Hardy, a partner in the Low Moor Company, who became one of Bradford's first two MPs; but soon after he left in 1824 the grounds and gardens at the rear of the hall were taken over for a market. The space in front, too, was commandeered by quack doctors and cheapjacks, and the narrow streets alongside became a shambles of shops and stalls. Lord Cranbrook, John Hardy's third son, who gave his name to Harold Park, would not have been proud to point to Goodchild's Temperance Hotel as his birthplace, but this was the use to which the Manor Hall had descended.

In 1866 the Council secured the market rights from the Rawsons, together with 18,000 square yards of land, a deal which led to the demolition of the Manor Hall and the erection of Kirkgate Market. The handsome Rawson Market

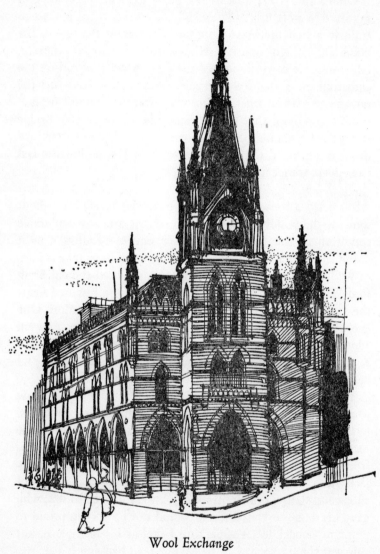

Wool Exchange

and the Open Market nearby completed a scheme which gave the public ample choice of shopping.

The Wool Exchange, which was completed in 1867, is a stately Gothic building where, on market days at "High change" business men from far and near assembled—one of the most remarkable sights in Bradford we are told. Looking down upon them, in the great hall, was the statue of Richard Cobden, the "Apostle of Free Trade". It was in 1842, to mark their appreciation of his policy, that the firm of Christopher Waud and Company made a gift of sufficient silk and alpaca material to make waistcoats for Cobden and three fellow MPs. It is said that during a debate on the Corn Laws Mr Cobden and his three friends exposed the waistcoats, with the word "Free" boldly displayed amid a design of wheat ears, to the full view of the House—"a sight to strike awe into the hearts of the Protectionists."

When the Corporation came into being it took over the Fire Station Building in Swaine Street and for twenty-six years these premises served as municipal offices. Here the Council held its regular meetings, but for larger gatherings either the Court House or the St George's Hall had to be used. Eventually it became obvious that official business ought to be conducted in a building more suited to the town's rising status, and after long debate the site for a Town Hall was chosen.

In a competition for the best design the award went to the local architects, Lockwood and Mawson, who had already distinguished themselves by erecting Saltaire Mills and the Wool Exchange. The style was Gothic, very much in favour at the time, and a feature of the design was a 220-foot tower modelled on the Campanile of the Palazzo Vecchio in Florence.

Once a decision on the design had been taken there was no delay. On 10 August 1870, a month after the tender had been accepted, Alderman Mark Dawson laid the foundation stone and three years later the Town Hall, completed at a cost of £100,000, was ready for opening.

Tuesday 9 September was declared a general holiday and a lengthy procession, including several bands, assembled at ten o'clock in the morning in Lister Park. Bradford's staple trade was naturally the central theme, Bishop Blaize being seated in state on one of the wagons, with sheep shearing and other live processes going on around him. The opening ceremony was performed by the Mayor, Alderman Matthew Thompson, to whom the procession brought back memories of 1825. He recalled how then, as a boy of five, he had been taught by his father to recite the St Blaize poem and placed on the top of a door, in full view of the crowd, to "spout the lines". His final hour of glory came when he was taken down into The Holme on a Shetland pony.

For several days after the opening, Bradford celebrated the occasion with galas, firework displays and illuminations, the Town Hall itself being "in the limelight" each evening.

Town Hall Opening Ceremony

11. TITUS SALT AND S. C. LISTER

The Town Hall had been open barely a year when workmen began to prepare a place for the statue of Sir Titus Salt in Market Street, only a short distance away. Titus Salt's connection with Bradford has been obscured by his achievements at Saltaire, but the nineteenth-century inhabitants of the town thought so much about him that they contributed £3,000 for a statue, which was erected during his lifetime.

The Salt family moved to Bradford from Wakefield when Titus was nineteen and his father apprenticed him to woolsorting. Having finished his training he became a partner in the firm of Daniel Salt and Son, and it was during his wool buying travels that he met his future wife, the youngest daughter of a rich Lincolnshire farmer, Mr Whitlam of Grimsby. The couple married in 1830 and set up house in Manor Row, a fashionable part of Bradford about a mile from the Listers at Manningham.

Titus Salt's first lone business venture was a near disaster. The purchase of a large quantity of Donskoi wool, the long, tangled fleece of a sheep which grazed on the banks of the Don—not in Yorkshire, but in Russia—stamped him as a man who was not afraid to take risks. His customers refused to buy the wool, so, with typical Bradford stubbornness he took over a mill in Silsbridge Lane—now Grattan Road—spun the Donskoi into excellent yarn and sold it without difficulty. What is more, the experience stood him in good stead, for it gave him an idea for dealing with the hair from the paca, or alpaca goat, an animal found high up on the Andes.

Mr Salt's second gamble has been given lively and imaginative treatment by Charles Dickens in *Household*

Words. Here, a plain-looking young business man stumbled upon three hundred or so bales of "superannuated horse hair", consigned to the firm of C. W. and F. Foozle and Co. Having tested the queer stuff, the young man returned to make an offer for the lot, but his bid of eightpence a pound so astonished Mr Foozle that he suspected his customer of being an escaped lunatic.

The true facts are that Mr Salt, seeing the unwanted bales in the warehouse, pulled out a sample of the hair and examined it carefully. On his next visit he took some of the hair home in a handkerchief and consulted his father, who strongly advised him not to touch it. Instead Titus bought the entire shipment. He then installed new machinery and spun

Titus Salt

and wove the hair into alpaca cloth, a strong, smooth, glossy material, which soon became fashionable at home and abroad.

Titus Salt did not discover alpaca in 1836, nor was he the first to make it into cloth—"Kit" Waud's, of Britannia Mills, claim to be the local pioneers. What he did was to establish a large industry which brought much trade into the country, so that within a few years 2,000,000 pounds of alpaca were being imported annually. Bradford, where the Salts had five or six mills, benefited greatly from the new trade. But the squalid conditions under which mill hands worked concerned Titus Salt so much that he resolved to move his factories away from the crowded centre of Bradford to a pleasant site by the River Aire at Shipley. Here he hoped his employees would lead healthier and better lives.

In 1847, the year of the Charter of Incorporation, Mr Salt, who had already been appointed Chief Constable, was made an alderman, and in the following year became Mayor and one of the town's leading magistrates.

A political opponent accused him of working for the incorporation of the town, and then removing his plant to Saltaire in order to avoid the heavy taxation which he knew would follow. Mr Lockwood, the architect of the "Palace of Industry", pointed out that at least three thousand Bradford men were employed during the building of the village and that, far from deserting the town, Mr Salt had placed contracts valued at a quarter of a million pounds with Bradford firms. The factory, designed in the Italian style, was a model of light and spaciousness, and in addition to the main building there were sheds covering several acres on either side. The mill was six storeys high, with a south front as long as that of St Paul's—545ft. And to show that no consideration was lacking, the Midland Railway passed within a few yards of the door.

The opening of Saltaire Mills was celebrated in 1853, on the owner's fiftieth birthday, when 3,500 people, most of them from the factory, sat down to a magnificent banquet in the combing shed.

Shipley Glen, only a mile or two from Bradford's smoking chimneys, is the town's nearest "resort"; a favourite place to former generations for week-end picnics and Sunday School outings. The walk from the tram stop at Victoria Road was through a village so spick and span that it was difficult to believe that people really lived there.

The houses—eight hundred and fifty in all—were revolutionary in their time. Lines of washing were forbidden in Saltaire. Instead, Mr Salt provided wash-houses with boiling-tubs into which steam and hot and cold water were conveyed in pipes. When the washing was done the clothes were put into wringing machines where the moisture was expelled by a strong current of air. Next they were placed in frames which ran on wheels into a drying closet heated with hot air. Within an hour the dirty clothes were washed, mangled, dried, and folded.

Regulations in Saltaire were strict. There must be no hoardings and no public houses. Titus Salt had seen so much of drunkenness in Bradford during his time as magistrate that he decided to put temptation out of reach. Instead he provided an Institute—the advantages of a pub without its evils—containing Reading Rooms, Library, Billiards Room and Gymnasium. Two huge lions, *War* and *Peace*, crouched outside the Institute, while across the road *Vigilance* and *Determination* kept watch over the Salt Schools.

The Salts, like many industrialists of the time, were staunch Nonconformists. After the move to Bradford they attached themselves to Horton Lane Congregational Chapel, where Titus, encouraged by James Garnett of Paper Hall, became first a Sunday School teacher and then Superintendent. At Saltaire he made wise provision for both body and soul, building forty-five almshouses complete with a chapel-of-ease, a Cottage Hospital, a magnificent Congregational Church and, in the belief that cleanliness comes next to godliness, twenty-four slipper baths and one Turkish bath.

The town continued to grow, until the owner wearied of hearing about the completion of Saltaire. For one who

planned to retire at fifty, Titus Salt's achievements were
incredible. He was often busily at work before the mill engine
started, a habit which gave rise to the legend that this
"persevering, plodding man" made a thousand pounds before
other manufacturers got out of bed. His initiative did not stop
at alpaca. The mills were noted for a great variety of fabrics,
including many kinds of worsted.

The Saltaire concern was founded on mutual respect
between master and workers. He gave security, fair conditions
and occasional trips into the country. They gave him service
and, as tokens of respect, a large bust of himself and a por-
trait.

On Mr Salt's fifty-third birthday three thousand "well-paid,
contented and happy operatives" headed by the Saltaire Drum
and Fife Band marched in procession, with flags and banners
flying, to the railway station *en route* for his home at
Lightcliffe. On arrival at *Crow Nest* the mill workers were
surprised to see in the grounds a flock of llamas, alpacas and
angora goats, animals whose hair was the means of much of
their livelihood. Hospitality was on the customary lavish scale
and the guests, seated at the tables in a monster marquee,
consumed huge amounts of food.

The presentation of the bust, carved by Mr Thomas Milnes,
took place in the evening at Bradford's new St George's Hall,
amid speeches, music and more refreshment. For Titus Salt
the task of improving the condition of the working classes
was, as he said, "not thankless or unprofitable".

It is estimated that Titus Salt gave away a quarter of a million
pounds, much of it without being asked. His bequests to good
causes in Bradford covered a very wide field; £11,000 for
scholarships at the two grammar schools; £1,000 towards the
cost of Peel Park and, a gift which caused some surprise,
£5,000 to help with the building of a "temporary" fever
hospital. These were official gifts, but personal need always
touched him very deeply and there are many stories of his
spontaneous generosity to those in distress.

Although distinctions inevitably came his way, Titus Salt was never very happy in the public gaze. He was elected MP for Bradford in 1859, but two years in Parliament were more than enough. To one used to regular hours—early to bed, early to rise—the long sittings were tedious and exhausting. His short parliamentary career, for which he was quite unsuited, seriously affected his health, and he retired so weary and broken that he thought his end had come. The bracing air of Scarborough revived him, however, and he lived to receive honours which weighed less heavily upon him.

In 1869 he became a baronet and four years later plans to erect a public statue were initiated. Unfortunately, one of the proposals inviting subscriptions fell into his hands and, after reading it through he is said to have remarked quietly, "So they wish to make me into a pillar of salt."

1 August 1874, the date of the unveiling of the statue, was a general holiday throughout the borough, and the ceremony, which was performed by the Duke of Devonshire, was attended by many dignitaries. The celebrations held afterwards in Peel Park were rounded off by a firework display, which included as a "set piece" *Bradford's Gratitude to Sir Titus Salt*. But the noise did not reach *Crow Nest*, where the subject of the rejoicing was passing his time quietly, no doubt tending his pineapples and other exotic fruits.

Two years after this Titus Salt died and the statue was draped in black. An immense funeral procession left the Town Hall for Shipley, and so many people lined the streets that a stranger might have been excused for thinking that a prince had passed away. Many thousands waited at the gates of the Congregational Church to pay their respects to the "Lord of Saltaire".

Saltaire, officially protected as a national monument, will keep the memory of its founder alive for generations to come, but another model village on a much smaller scale, Ripleyville, became derelict in 1970.

In 1863 Henry Ripley, son of George Ripley, who founded Bowling Dyeworks, built two hundred houses for his

employees in six not very impressive terraces. His idea was
that tenants should eventually buy the houses they lived in,
but the scheme failed because the workpeople did not like
being tied down to one place.

Henry Ripley, who, like Titus Salt, was made a baronet,
provided schools, which he maintained for a time at his own
expense. He brought the number of almshouses up to ten and
also gave the site for St Bartholomew's Church. But Ripleyville did not survive the rapid changes which took place after
the Second World War. Bowling was not Saltaire. The
neighbourhood deteriorated and, worst of all, Edward Ripley
and Sons, a firm with a world-wide reputation, lost its trade
and closed down.

Titus Salt and Samuel Cunliffe Lister seem to monopolise the
mid-nineteenth century industrial scene in Bradford; indeed,
the latter was a dominating figure for over fifty years. One
hard earned fortune, followed by retirement, would have been
enough for most men, but when he had mastered the combing
machine Lister looked round for new worlds to conquer, and
stumbled upon silk.

Walking through a London warehouse one day in 1855,
with his eyes very much on the ground, he came across an
interesting pile of rubbish containing,

> bits of stick, dead leaves, ends of twine, dirty flocks, crushed
> worms and silk fibres, all stuck together by gummy matter;

and from these poor beginnings sprang the largest silk mill in
Europe.

The story of his success with silk waste has the same fairy
tale element as Titus Salt's adventures with alpaca, but the
rubbish Lister began with was even less promising than the
stuff which attracted Titus Salt's attention in Liverpool. It
had been tried as manure but without results, and if Samuel
Lister had known the expense in which he was about to be
involved he would have thrown the "Native Indian Chassum"
into the Thames. As it was, the owner was glad to get rid of

it for a halfpenny a pound, and at this price the waste was transferred to Manningham. Yet this unlikely material, supplemented by silk from the Lister estates in India, formed the basis of the vast production at Manningham Mills.

However, before he had made as much as a shilling from his silk machines, Samuel Lister was a quarter of a million pounds out of pocket. And just when success seemed likely, the Old Mill was burned to the ground. Few men could have survived disaster on such a scale, but the fire merely cleared the way for a bigger and more impressive factory. In ten years the profits from the silk comb, which Lister perfected, rebuilt and refurnished Manningham Mills, and made a large contribution towards developing the velvet loom.

Profits are seldom made without trouble and some of the most serious riots ever known in Bradford came at the end of a long strike by over four thousand employees at Lister's. Their protest was against a considerable reduction in wages brought about by a slump in trade. The hands were determined not to accept the cuts, but they were up against a man who was prepared to close the mill down and ship it to America rather than give in.

For nearly five months the strike dragged on, until one night, on 12 April 1891, after a crowded meeting in St George's Hall, scuffles with the police took place. The following night was ominous as twenty thousand people, defying a ban, gathered in Town Hall Square. Setts were prized up, stones thrown and, after the Chief Constable had been injured, a detachment of troops helped to break up the mobs.

The third night provided a spectacular climax. Because hooligans had smashed the street lamps a searchlight was placed on the Town Hall tower and, as the crowds gathered again, they were met by troops and mounted police, who quickly cleared the square. After a few more baton charges order was restored and the strikers, beaten and broken, returned to work on the master's terms.

The troubles at Lister's are said to have given birth to the Independent Labour Party, which held a conference in Brad-

Riot outside St George's Hall

ford in 1893. Among those present on this occasion were George Bernard Shaw, Keir Hardie—the first Socialist MP—and Fred Jowett, who became a Minister in the 1924 Labour Government.

Manningham Park, the old home of the Lister family, was offered by Samuel Lister to the Corporation in 1870 at the bargain price of £40,000—much less than it was worth. In 1898 he put forward a proposal to build the Cartwright Memorial Hall in the park, at the price paid for the estate, but this amount proved to be inadequate and a further sum was added.

The architect provided Bradford with the kind of memorial it had come to expect—solid, massive and splendidly decorated. The hall, which was built of stone from the Idle Quarries, stood foursquare on the old engine bed stones from Lister's Mill, and at the entrance to the park Bradford woolmen placed a statue of Lister, long after he had ceased to deal in wool.

12. EDUCATION

Before the Wool Exchange was built, Bradford merchants concluded their deals at the Old Exchange, Piccadilly, a short distance from the new building. Here, on a certain market day in 1841, serious business was disturbed by a tall young man of somewhat curious appearance, who bounded up the steps two or three at a time, pushed open the door, and shouldered his way through the crowds in search of a customer. Word soon got round that this was Thomas Fison's new partner from somewhere outside the town. He certainly wasn't a Yorkshireman, and there was a rumour that he liked books, a trait which placed him under even more suspicion. In fact, William Edward Forster, the young man concerned, was a native of Bradpole in Dorsetshire. He learnt to weave at Norwich and then picked up woolsorting in a factory at Darlington. Now he was in the woolstapling business with Thomas Fison.

It was a few years before this that William Forster senior, a Quaker missionary, went north from Bradpole, in Dorsetshire, to preach the gospel, and found himself in the same coach as Thomas Fison, head of the woolstapling firm of James Fison and Son, Thetford. During conversation Mr Forster voiced his anxiety about his son's future, and later, after some correspondence, it was decided that William Edward Forster should join James's son, Thomas, who was a woolstapler in Bradford.

Soon after coming to Bradford Forster struck up a friendship with another member of the Fison family, William, and entered into partnership with him as a manufacturer. Their first factory, Waterloo Mill, stood on the site once occupied by Swan Arcade. Eventually Forster withdrew from wool-stapling altogether, and in 1850 he and William Fison moved their manufacturing business to Burley-in-Wharfedale. It was in this year, too, that Forster married Jane, the eldest daughter of the Rev. Thomas Arnold—the famous Dr Arnold of Rugby. With such a father, Jane was, as might be expected, a member of the Church of England, but her husband was a Quaker.

Before the wedding took place, a deputation of Quakers went to tell Forster, at his home at Rawdon, that the mixed marriage would bring about his expulsion from their congregation. Having delivered their message the members of the deputation warmly congratulated the future bridegroom upon his choice of such an eligible partner. Some time afterwards Forster, who had joined the Church of England, told his Quaker friends, "Your people turned me out of the Society for doing the best thing I ever did in my life." Two years after their marriage the Forsters moved to Burley, and *Wharfeside*, the gabled house they built overlooking the river, became their home for the rest of their lives.

As a young man William had helped his uncle, a retired MP, to prepare documents for submission to the Government on the subject of the effects of the Slave Trade in Africa, and he was ready to sail with an expedition to the Niger if he had been allowed to go. Human suffering concerned him deeply. Twice during the potato famine he visited Ireland to see what conditions were like and to administer relief provided by the Quakers in England. He was determined to do some good in the world and a career in public life seemed ear-marked for him.

Industrial Bradford presented Forster with golden opportunities for social service, and he was voted on to committees of all kinds. He supported the aims of the Chartists but not their violence, and he and Thomas Cooper, one of their leaders, became firm friends. In 1848, when law and order were seriously threatened, the poor looked to Forster as their champion. On returning to Bradford from a visit to France he described the scenes that met him—the Chartist riots.

Night drilling, pike buying, monster meetings, troops of soldiers, and, of course, a bitter class feeling. But also . . . a growing sense among the upper classes that they must, for their own sakes, stop the starving of the labourer.

As a special constable he found himself in danger of being stoned and clubbed by those he was trying to help; "hooted by one party and abused by the other". His course and his conscience were clear, however. He must help the people to obtain their due by peaceful means.

Throughout the nineteenth century education was a burning question, and long before he married into the Arnold family Forster was heard to say again and again :

If I had to take part in the administration of affairs in this country I would strive to accomplish two great purposes—to give relief, and lasting relief, to poor Ireland; and to get the children of the working classes out of the gutter by educating them.

In the scramble to provide some form of education for children who worked six days a week, Sunday Schools emerged as a possible solution. In the early part of the nineteenth century the Bradford Parish Church had three or four such schools, one of them being held in the Old Market Hall. Christ Church was built in 1815, at the top of Darley Street, and a Sunday School was opened in Westgate. It was from this school that Bradford's first Church of England Day school developed in 1831.

Parson Bull, the Curate of Bierley, was a keen promoter of Sunday Schools but he found, as others did, that before any progress could be made teachers had to combat the dirt, ignorance and almost savage rudeness of their unwilling pupils. They also had to contend with the perpetual tiredness of their charges but, after six days of early rising, the wonder is that children attended classes at all on their day of rest.

By 1843 there were about eighty-eight Sunday Schools in Bradford, most of them attached to Nonconformist places of

worship. This movement owed much, however, to the efforts
of the Vicar of Bradford, the Rev. Henry Heap who, in 1828,
erected a special building in Stott Hill for use as a Sunday
School. The classes formerly held in the Old Market Hall were
transferred to the new building, and the Parish Church Sunday School became the largest of its kind in the town. Mr
Heap, who did much good work during the strike of 1825,
was succeeded by Dr William Scoresby, one of the most
remarkable men of his day.

William Scoresby was the son of a Whitby seaman
employed in the northern whaling industry. As a youth he
accompanied his father on eight expeditions, and on his
twentieth birthday was appointed to the command of the
Resolution in his father's place. After making many voyages
to the Arctic he left the sea and entered Cambridge to read
for the ministry, being ordained in 1825. A curacy at Brid-
lington gave him leisure to pursue his studies, not in theology
but in whaling, and there he published his book on the Arctic
Regions.

Dr Scoresby came to Bradford at the age of 35, just before
William Forster, and stayed for eight unhappy years. He fell
foul of the mill owners because he took the children's side
against them and incurred the wrath of Nonconformists by
trying to levy a church rate. He was distressed to find that
among all the families under his care not one child was
receiving day-time education, a state of affairs he was determined to put right. The great need was money, which he
raised by addressing public meetings, not only in Bradford but
up and down the country. Most important of all, perhaps, was
the contribution he himself made, for he is said to have
given every penny of his stipend to this and other good
causes.

As a result of his efforts, four new day schools were opened
and five others already in existence incorporated into his
scheme. In the midst of all the cares of a large parish, Dr
Scoresby found time to devote himself whole-heartedly to the
education of poor children. Yet, in spite of all his efforts, his

ministry was not a success, and he left Bradford in 1846, an ailing, disillusioned man.

Among the voluntary efforts to provide education, benevolent factory owners played a part. The Low Moor Company carried on the good work begun by Joseph Dawson, opening a day school in 1814. This continued as Low Moor Church School until the 1970s. The Bowling Iron Company also provided a room in which a day school was run in connection with St John's Church. Wood's spinning mill, in the Bridge Street area, was the largest in the town, employing 3,000 hands, of whom 500 were young children, and it was here that Oastler's friend opened one of the most famous factory schools in the country.

Wood operated a ten hour day long before it became law, and employed extra workers so that the children in the mill could be relieved to attend school. One of the Rev. G. S. Bull's pupils, Matthew Balme, was appointed as master of Wood's school, which gained a high reputation under his supervision. William Walker, who was taken into partnership by Wood in 1835, was connected with the firm for thirty-two years, during which time he continued its enlightened policies.

John Wood left Bradford in 1837, but before he went laid the foundation stone of St James's Church, Manchester Road, which he built and endowed, along with its school and vicarage. Parson Bull was the first incumbent, and he and Walker were associated with Wood and Richard Oastler as "Distinguished Advocates" of the Ten Hours Bill, which was passed in 1847. Three years before this, William Walker took over the tenancy of Bolling Hall and was host to Lord Ashley —when he toured factories in the north. "Walker's Factory School" remained in existence until about 1873, but the company's land had been sold earlier for development by the Lancashire and Yorkshire Railway.

Praiseworthy as these voluntary efforts were, they did no more than scratch the surface of the educational problem. In Bradford, with its swarms of ragged children, the need for a proper system of education was desperate, a fact which no one felt more deeply than W. E. Forster. On 2 May 1850, he addressed a meeting in the Temperance Hall, which was filled to overflowing with an enthusiastic audience. In his speech Forster moved a resolution urging Parliament to meet the situation by devising a national system, which would come, as far as possible, under local control.

In 1859 the opportunity for which Forster had waited so long came. He was invited to stand as one of the Liberal candidates for Leeds at the General Election, but on this occasion he was defeated by a small majority. Two years later, however, upon the resignation of Titus Salt, Forster was returned unopposed as one of the Members for Bradford, a seat he held until his death.

In 1865 Forster became Under-Secretary for the Colonies and three years later was made Vice-President of the Council: "in other words", as Wemyss Reid, Forster's biographer says, "he became Minister of Education in the reformed Parliament." Education was not his only care, however: the new post, by some strange chance, made him responsible for both the children of the country and its cattle. So, in 1869, when his mind was fully occupied with the problem of the nation's schooling, Forster, as Reid tells us, "had to spend no small portion of his time in coping with an outbreak of cattle disease, and in passing a measure designed to stamp out threatened plague."

One of Forster's first tasks after taking office was to see the *Endowed Schools Act* of 1839 safely through all its stages. Many of the "middle class" grammar schools were in an unsatisfactory state, and this Act aimed at setting them on a better footing. Bradford's own grammar school was in existence before 1553, but its official constitution dates from the Restoration, when it was granted a Charter, and became known as the "Free Grammar School of King Charles the Second at Bradford". Many distinguished men owed their early education to this school, among them John Sharp, who became Archbishop of York, Abraham Sharp, the mathematician and astronomer, and Dr Richard Richardson of Bierley Hall. Joseph Lister, who wrote the "Genuine Account" of the siege of Bradford, also attended the grammar school.

By the middle of the nineteenth century, however, the school had deteriorated, and its forty-two pupils, we are told, learned little or nothing. In fact, much of its work had been taken over by the Bradford High School, an institution founded by Sir Jacob Behrens and other business men, for the purpose of ensuring a good education for their sons.

Old Grammar School

In 1871 permission was granted to erect a new grammar school, and before the building was ready, staff and boys joined in lessons with the High School on their premises in Hallfield Road. Then, in 1873, when the school in Manor Row was completed, the High School and Bradford Grammar School became one, under the headship of the Rev. W. H. Keeling. The re-formed school was one of the first to feel the benefits of the 1869 Act, and its modern history dates from this period. It was opened, very appropriately, by the Rt Hon W. E. Forster in July, 1873, and since that date the school has maintained a high national reputation, educating generations of distinguished scholars.

Until the "new-scheme", as the 1869 Act was called, came into force, little thought had been given to the higher education of girls. In Bradford, advantage was taken of the far-sighted provisions made by Forster to found a girls' grammar school, which was opened in 1875, a worthy counterpart to that of the boys. The Bradford Girls' Grammar School first occupied premises in Hallfield Road, only a short distance from Manor Row.

Just when Forster's political career seemed assured a scandal occurred which threatened to ruin him. In the General Election of 1868 Edward Miall, Forster's fellow Liberal, was defeated by Henry Ripley, but complaints were made that Mr Ripley had bribed his supporters, especially the Irish labourers, by giving them free beer. His election expenses were over £7,000, an enormous sum, and when the case came before Judge Baron Martin the verdict went against Mr Ripley.

By way of revenge Ripley's supporters petitioned against Forster, on the grounds that his campaign had been conducted dishonestly. The decision was awaited eagerly by crowds outside the Court House, and when it became known that Forster had been cleared the roar drowned the judge's closing speech. At Burley a torchlight procession formed up, and the whole population turned out to welcome the hero home.

Forster's greatest moment came on 17 February 1870, when he explained to the House of Commons his proposals for bringing the benefits of education to every child in England and Wales, irrespective of position or class. In brief, his plan was to provide good schools in all districts and persuade parents to send their children to them. The big problem was the voluntary schools, especially those belonging to the Church of England. Many of the people Forster represented in Bradford wanted to see the end of Church Schools, but he proposed to make the best use he could of them and then, as he put it, "fill up the gaps". For this purpose each district was asked to take stock of its schools and decide how many more would be needed to provide a place for every child. Where the number of schools was inadequate, School Boards were to be elected, and it was their job to provide the extra accommodation.

Forster's proposals were not new. Many of them had been made before by others, but prolonged and bitter arguments had wrecked all previous attempts to reach a solution. He succeeded because, although he gave way on some points, he refused to accept delay. He said, in effect, "Get the children into school and argue later." For five months the Education Bill was the subject of fierce debate, but on 9 August 1870 the Act became law.

When Forster met his constituents at a crowded meeting in St George's Hall a motion expressing disapproval of the Education Act was carried by a small majority. His reply left the audience in no doubt what he thought about them.

> "You have only done what I have always expected Bradford people to do—to say what you think. Still I believe the time will come, and that before long, when many of you will regret much that expression of opinion."

It must have given him great satisfaction later, to see his adopted town taking the lead in putting the Act into practice, and becoming a pioneer in promoting the welfare and education of children.

Shortly before 1870 Forster, who had a hand in most educational enterprises, advocated a technical university to counteract the demand for French cloths, which had caused a slump in Bradford after the Paris Exhibition of 1867. His suggestion was not adopted, but the general need to improve both the quality and design of Bradford goods led to the founding of the Technical College. It began as a Technical School in the Mechanics' Institute, but became independent in 1882, when the Prince and Princess of Wales opened the new premises in Great Horton Road. This was a great occasion for the town, entailing the most elaborate preparations, and to commemorate the royal visit the "Norman Arch" was erected at Lister Park.

Since then, the Technical College has been the recognized

training ground for all branches of the textile industry, although its courses have not been confined to that trade alone. Long before Bradford had a university the "Tech" gained an international reputation, and overseas students have always formed part of its intake.

Many unkind things were said about W. E. Forster. He was described by some as "stubborn", "graceless" and "defiant", even as a "stage Yorkshireman", but to others he was "honest", "courageous" and "sympathetic". The truth seems to lie between the two opinions. Above all he was a man of action, and his great physical energy was soon noticed in Bradford, where a mason once told a lazy apprentice to be like "Long" Forster, who "walked to Colne and back"—a distance of thirty miles—"before breakfast".

When the Liberal Government was defeated at the General Election of 1874, Forster had to resign from office, although he still retained his seat. He quickly took advantage of the spell of freedom, first to visit America, and then to make a tour of the Near East. During an interval between his journeyings he received the freedom of Edinburgh and was elected Lord Rector of Aberdeen University.

The year 1880 found him once more in office, as Chief Secretary for Ireland, where his forthright manner earned him the name of "Buckshot" from the Irish newspapers. The sympathetic side of his character was displayed, however, in attempts to get large quantities of seed potatoes to the starving peasants.

In spite of the great demands upon his time throughout the years, Forster was present at most of Bradford's important civic functions. He spoke at the unveiling of statues to Peel and Oastler; he opened the new Mechanics' Institute and the Bradford Grammar School building, and he also unveiled the statue to Samuel Cunliffe Lister in Manningham Park.

Forster died on 5 April 1886. Bradford honoured him with a statue and named Forster Square after him; but the town he represented paid its greatest tribute to his memory by the zeal it showed for education, and by the reputation it gained as a pioneer among local authorities.

The inscription at the base of Forster's statue in London is simply, dignified and true:

> To his wisdom and courage England owes the establishment throughout the land of a national system of elementary education.

Bradford was quick to comply with the terms of the 1870 Education Act and before the end of that year a School Board had been elected. "Stocktaking" revealed that although the population had risen from about 66,000 in 1841 to 145,000 in 1871 the town was very well provided with voluntary schools. Nevertheless, by 1874 eight Board Schools had been completed, Bowling Back Lane being the first to open.

After nearly a hundred years, many of these buildings with their towers and turrets, more like places of worship than schools, are still in use. They could have been built at half the cost, without being inadequate, but the architects were out to impress, and so much attention was paid to appearances that utility was often overlooked. The pace of building did not slacken and by 1885 the town had an impressive total of twenty-one Board schools.

The Bradford Board, forward-looking in spite of immense problems, set up a record in 1897, with the first school swimming pool in England, at Wapping Road, a bath which still serves a very useful purpose. A less enviable record, however, was Bradford's total of half-timers, the largest in the country. These were children who, after working at the mill for six hours in the morning, attended school to nod at their desks in the afternoon.

There was a danger that School Boards would concern themselves entirely with education of the most elementary kind, but this was not the case in Bradford. James Hanson, who was elected by working men to the first Board, began as a mill hand at eight years of age, but by dint of much self-help became a teacher and eventually the principal of a flourishing private school. It was Hanson, along with others, who turned Bradford's attention, illegally as it happened, to secondary education, giving the town the first higher grade school in the country—Feversham Street—and no fewer than six similar schools out of a national total of sixty by 1903. The Bryce Commission's report that "a door is open in Bradford for a boy of special ability to pass right through to the Universities" must have been proudly received, for it was no small thing in 1895.

One Bradford boy of very special ability got to University without the help of any regular schooling. At the age of six Joseph Wright began work as a "donkey-boy" in a quarry. In 1862, when he was seven, he left and went to Salt's Mill, where he attended the master's special school for half-timers. His real education, however, began at the Bradford Mechanics' Institute and continued at the Yorkshire College, Leeds.

Joseph Wright's industry was phenomenal. All the classes were held in the evening, and he thought nothing of walking from Thackley to Leeds and back after a hard day's work. His wife tells how he often sat up until two in the morning and still managed to be at the mill before six. Eventually he was admitted to Heidelberg University, where he took his doctorate in 1885. In 1891 he began to compile the *English Dialect Dictionary*, a task which took fourteen years to complete, and in 1901 the ex-donkey boy and doffer was appointed Professor of Comparative Philology at Oxford, a post he held until 1924.

Nowhere was the battle against ignorance and poverty carried on with more vigour than in the early Roman Catholic schools. The log books kept by head teachers tell an almost monotonous tale of dirt, disease and truancy. St Patrick's was closed in 1874 because of an epidemic of smallpox, followed by measles, and the log book entry ends poignantly, "young children dying daily". The fight was sometimes against parents who seemed to care little what their children did; but when "Mr Mullins gave clogs and stockings to all poor children in need of them", St Ann's had a full turn up.

All Roman Catholic schools sprang from St Mary's on the Mount, established as a parish church in 1825, and, although money was very difficult to raise, no schools were handed over to the Bradford Board in 1870. Little expansion was possible until after the Second World War, but thereafter the story is one of immense effort, resulting in a succession of modern, well equipped schools for all ages.

St Bede's Grammar School began life in 1900 at a house in Drewton Street, off Manningham Lane. The roll consisted of thirty-seven boys under the care of two priests who were both to become famous in very different ways. Dr Hinsley, the headmaster, became Cardinal Archbishop of Westminster, and his assistant, the small, cheerful, Father O'Connor, went down to posterity as "Father Brown". G. K. Chesterton and Father —later Monsignor—O'Connor were personal friends, and through their association the priest gained a place in fiction as the aimiable amateur detective of the *Father Brown Stories*. One of the volumes is dedicated to:

> Father John O'Connor of St Cuthbert's, Bradford, whose truth is stranger than fiction; with a gratitude greater than the world.

St Joseph's College, the corresponding school for girls, formed originally as a pupil teacher centre, was opened officially in 1908.

Since those early days both schools have expanded continuously, taking in scholars not only from Bradford but from the surrounding districts, too.

In November 1893 Margaret McMillan and her sister Rachel arrived in Bradford from London. It was a stormy night and as they left the Midland Station they saw, through a flurry of rain, the shining statue of Richard Oastler and the two factory children. If they had been able to see a little further they would have noticed another figure, that of W. E. Forster, raising a hand towards them. Margaret

McMillan would have been astonished if she had known that before long she, too, would go down in history as a great reformer, honoured by three memorials in Bradford alone: a College of Education, the McMillan School and the McMillan Community Centre.

Margaret McMillan had come to Bradford at the request of Fred Jowett and others to help with the work of the Independent Labour Party, which had its headquarters in the town. Miss McMillan's distinctly middle-class upbringing did not appear to fit her for the task of dealing with the tough, working people of Bradford. She was born in America, and when Margaret's father died Mrs McMillan returned, with her two young daughters, to their home in Scotland. After studying music in Germany, Margaret returned to work as a governess in Scotland, where she became interested in Socialism. Her next move was to London, where she combined speaking from Socialist platforms with her duties as a lady's companion.

Margaret McMillan was an accomplished linguist, but the fact that she had not been trained to teach, and had no experience in school management, did not indicate a future for her as an educational reformer. She was shocked, however, by the condition of the children in Bradford. It was clear that the 1870 Act had worked no miracles. There had been plenty of building, but "bricks and mortar" did not impress Miss McMillan. She saw the half-timers asleep over their lessons and little children in all stages of misery, and decided to take up their cause. She kept to her word, and conducted her campaign at all times and in all places. She was as much at home speaking at street corners, accompanied by Charlie the Bellman, as at crowded meetings in the St George's Hall.

When she was elected to the School Board—the youngest member and the only woman—in 1894, Margaret McMillan declared her intention of fighting the battle of the slum child. Health came first on her list of priorities, and here she found a valuable ally in Dr James Kerr who, without official permission, had been appointed School Medical Officer. In fact,

much of Bradford's pioneer work—the "zeal for education"
—brought little approval from the Government of the
day.

The first systematic school medical inspection ever to be
held in the country took place at Usher Street in 1899. For
three days Margaret McMillan sat, watched and made notes,
as Dr Kerr examined 285 girls. The results were so disturbing
that a public meeting was called to let parents know how bad
things really were. On another occasion it was discovered that
over a hundred children had not had their clothes off for six
or seven months. Fumigating stations were set up, and where
clothing had to be burnt supplies were provided by charitable
organizations.

This was the beginning of the School Health Service in
Bradford, so much ahead of its time that in 1910 the following
report was received from the Board of Education.

> The school clinic at Bradford is the most complete in
> England and has achieved a large amount of pioneer work,
> which has been of the utmost value as a model to many
> other Education Authorities throughout the country.

Margaret McMillan was only in Bradford for nine years,
but her influence was profound and lasting. She attacked evil
at the roots, her belief being that it was impossible to educate
dirty, ailing and neglected children. She regarded fresh air
and water as the best friends a child could have, and for this
reason pressed for the school bath at Wapping, where she got
her way.

On one occasion, at least, Margaret McMillan's passion for
cleanliness had unfortunate results. A story is told that in one
school where there were no facilities she got an old, leaking
bath; plugged it; painted it white and, later in the day, bathed
a dirty little girl in it. Unfortunately the paint was not quite
dry, and the poor child ended up whiter in parts than she
should have been.

Margaret McMillan campaigned for so much that we now
take for granted:

for more hygienic school buildings, for lectures on child health, for lessons in voice production, for an extra full year at school for half-timers, for Kindergarten methods in infant schools, for free Saturdays for pupil teachers and for better facilities for handicapped children.

In Bradford she made both enemies and friends. The employers, for instance, and some parents, were bitterly opposed to her attempts to put an end to the half-time system, but for others she could do no wrong. The best and simplest testimonial came in a letter to the local paper:

I voted Church last time, but next time I shall plump for Miss McMillan. She looks after the poor.

When Margaret McMillan first came to Bradford many people assumed that she was "well off". In fact, she had very little money, and as she was unpaid, her sister had to help to keep her from the salary she earned as a sanitary inspector. In 1902, when Margaret's health failed, she left Bradford, "the city of my heart", to live with Rachel in Kent. The convalescence, however, was only a prelude to further activity and international fame as an educational pioneer, for which services she was made a C.B.E. in 1917 and a Companion of Honour in 1930.

In Bradford Margaret McMillan's name is especially remembered for the help she gave in establishing nurseries. She and her sister became convinced that the early years were the most important ones in a child's life—that the first years decide all. Rachel opened her own nursery and teacher training centre at Deptford during the First World War, and many Bradford teachers went there for instruction. Margaret kept in touch with Bradford and spoke at the opening of St Ann's Nursery in 1920. Later she had much to do with setting the pattern for Bradford's first two purpose-built nursery schools.

The McMillan sisters and the Bradford Education Committee were among the leaders of the movement to provide school meals for needy children. As a result of deputations to the Government, an Act came into force in 1906 which permitted Education Committees to supply meals where it was thought necessary. Already in Bradford 450 poor children were receiving meals daily through the Board of Guardians, and now this task was taken over by the Committee. By way of an experiment, about forty of these children were given three meals a day, during the summer of 1907, at the expense of the Lord Mayor. At the same time, a central cooking depot was being built at Green Lane School, where Jonathan Priestley, the father of J. B. Priestley, was head teacher. From this depot, believed to be the first of its kind in the country, dinners were despatched in special containers to various dining centres—the start of a regular school meals service.

13. MODERN BRADFORD

From about 1850 Bradford went through a period of rapid building which stamped it as a "Victorian" town. The scene was set, as it were, by the completion of St George's Hall—albeit in Leeds stone. This was followed in 1855 by the first of Bradford's large statues to eminent men, Sir Robert Peel, who abolished the Corn Laws. Bradford's first park, opened in 1863, was also named after him.

One by one the large civic buildings were erected, together with many impressive places of worship. The charge that the Church of England had neglected its flock was put right by the provision of ten churches in twelve years, between 1860 and 1872, after which the pace slackened a little. The School Board, when its turn came, was far from negligent, and by 1903, when it ceased to exist, had built fifty-six schools, with all the necessary adjuncts.

In addition, huge sums were spent on street widening, drainage and general improvements; £3,000,000 being the cost of water projects which culminated in the Nidd Valley scheme. The purchase and demolition of the Queen's Mill (the old Soke Mill) and the construction of Sunbridge Road was one of the Corporation's most ambitious tasks.

In 1882 the Broadstones area was cleared to make way for Forster Square, with a new Midland Station and a Post Office placed in front of the Parish Church, where it obscured the impressive ascent to the west door. Since then, "moving the Post Office" has been a recurring theme in all discussions about plans for this part of the town.

Stone quarrying was such a thriving industry that Bradford, besides meeting its own heavy demands and supplying other towns, sent consignments abroad, even as far as Australia. In fact, trade was so good that in 1870 a *Stone Exchange* was contemplated. This did not materialize, but unlike coal mining "stone-getting" never quite died out, and a few quarries are working at the present time.

These were years of phenomenal growth, and by 1891 the population of Bradford had risen to over 216,000. To meet the needs of the workers and their families regulations were relaxed to permit, once again, the construction of large numbers of back-to-back houses. This type of accommodation was not finally banned until 1900, by which time substantial better-class terrace houses were being erected in all parts of the town. One of the thriving districts was Lilycroft, at the centre of which stood the new Board School and Lister's massive new mill, which had been built to replace the old one destroyed by fire in 1871.

Bradford's rising importance was acknowledged by the grant of city status in 1897, and Samuel Cunliffe Lister, who had become Lord Masham six years earlier, was given final recognition at home by being made a Freeman of the city in 1898. Before the end of the nineteenth century all the townships which make up the present city, with the exception of Esholt and Clayton, had been incorporated into it.

Lord Masham, the city's second Freeman, heralded the twentieth century in Bradford by laying the foundation stone of the Cartwright Memorial Hall. Four years later, in 1904, he performed the opening ceremony.

In the following May, the whole population turned out to give a magnificent welcome to the Prince and Princess of Wales, the future King George V and Queen Mary, when they came to open the Bradford Exhibition in Manningham Park. The Exhibition, which lasted until November, was a tremendous success. Besides the specially built pavilion for the display of industrial products there was a concert hall, and by far the biggest attraction for the 2,500,000 visitors, a Somali village peopled by natives. Other entertainments included a Crystal Maze, and on the lake, which had been constructed by unemployed men some twenty years before, a Naval Spectacle was held. On the day of the opening the Prince of Wales unveiled the statue of Queen Victoria, which stands between Morley Street and Little Horton Lane, and the royal tour also included a visit to Lister's mill.

Earlier that year the City Council took a decision to buy the Esholt estate from the Misses Crompton Stansfield, a transaction with a considerable history behind it.

Esholt, formerly a beautiful, wooded spot, lies on a bend of the Aire overlooked by Idle Hill, about four miles north of Bradford. Here, with an eye for seclusion, a community of Cistercian nuns settled in the thirteenth century. When they were dispossessed by Henry VIII a mansion was built on the site, to be replaced later by Esholt Hall, which became the home of the Stansfield family. But one day in 1861 Mr William Rookes Crompton Stansfield, the owner of the hall, drove down the fine avenue of elms for the last time. He was turning his back on progress.

The construction of the Midland Railway in 1846 had earned his severe disapproval, but the newly proposed Otley–Ilkley line was more than he could stand. Nor was this all. On his way to Frimley Park, Surrey, he cursed both the railways and the wretches who had ruined his fishing by pouring their filth into the River Aire. He was unable to stop the trains, but he would get even with the mill owners. In 1868 he took legal action against the Bradford Corporation to prevent further pollution of the river, and his case was upheld.

History took strange revenge. Bradford, having failed to dispose of the sewage from its mills satisfactorily elsewhere, decided that Esholt, after all, was the only place for it. As a result, the Council purchased the estate, and in this quiet haven made preparations for fifty-three acres of filter beds, driving a tunnel into Idle Hill big enough for a car to pass through.

The Esholt Works constitute one of the minor wonders of

the industrial world; and what is more, they uphold the Bradfordian creed, "Where there's muck, there's brass", for by-products, especially garden fertilizer, bring in thousands of pounds each year.

One of the great events of the late nineteenth century was the introduction of tramcars. In Bradford, rails were laid from Darley Street to Manningham Park and trams, pulled by teams of ten horses, kept a half-hourly service going. Steam trams were already being considered, however, and they were soon running about the town at speeds of up to twelve miles an hour—a pace described as "too great to be tolerated". By 1909 a through service was in operation between Leeds and Bradford. Two years later Bradford made history by putting into operation the first trackless service in the country, beating Leeds by a few hours. Having pinned its faith on trolley buses Bradford stood by them to the very end, for on Sunday 26 March 1972 enthusiasts from all over the country gathered in the city to witness the ceremonial closure of the last trolley bus service in the British Isles.

Bradford was criticized in the nineteenth century for not being "theatre minded" although amateur dramatic societies have always flourished in the town. It is not surprising, however, that men and women who "grafted" in a mill were in no mood for serious plays at the end of a long day—but they knew how to enjoy themselves. Travelling shows, circuses and strolling players visited the town, and fairs, tides and galas were usually great attractions. Music hall entertainment was also very popular.

Nevertheless, we hear, in 1820, of "Thompson's Theatre", in a building called Bartle's Corner in Market Street, where a play called The Siege of Bradford was performed with some success. Next followed "Smedley's", a large wooden theatre, near Peel Square. Here, between the intervals of serious plays, the "stars" had to sing, to the best of their ability, songs like "Has your mother sold her mangle?" Even the great Lysander Thompson was not spared the humiliation of singing a piece with the curious title "The Improvements of Bradford, or a Peep at the Wool Trade".

A temporary circus building in Duke Street was altered, improved and given a "grand new front", to a design which incorporated the old stone gate posts from the Manor Hall. It was then reopened and proudly named the "Theatre Royal", which it remained until 1867. Bradford had no really permanent theatre until 1864, when the Royal Alexandra opened in Manningham Lane; and when the old Theatre Royal closed down it took over that name. The "Royal", now used as a cinema, was a fine theatre which attracted many famous actors in its day. On 13 October 1905 Sir Henry Irving made a tragic last appearance there, in a play called *Becket*. After the performance he returned to his rooms at the Midland Hotel, where he was taken ill suddenly, and died.

The completion of the Alhambra in 1914 gave Bradford its fifth theatre, but the opening of cinemas, and the invention of talkies and television, caused them to close down one by one. Finally, the Alhambra, the lone survivor, was taken over by the Corporation, but even this theatre was struggling for existence in 1972.

In 1929, just as talking films were making an entry, Bradford embarked upon a small but significant venture. With the help and example of Leeds, a Civic Playhouse was inaugurated, the initial meeting being held at the home of the Priestley family.

Although "Jack" Boynton Priestley had not really lived in Bradford since the days when he worked as an unwilling clerk for a wool merchant in Swan Arcade, he always retained an affection for the smoky, homely city he knew before the war. He attended the first meeting of the proposed Playhouse and became its president, an office he held for twenty-five years. His sister was the first secretary.

The Jowett Hall, in Chapel Street, where performances were given, was burnt down in 1935, but under the chairmanship of Thomas Boyce, the Director of Education, money was raised and a new theatre with seating for about 300, was built

on the same site. Since then, even throughout the Second
World War, a varied programme of plays has been presented
every year.

A drama school was opened in 1946, under the direction of
Esmé Church, where young people could be trained for the
professional stage. Billie Whitelaw appeared as a child actor
at the "Civic", and Peter Dews, who produced *The Age of
Kings* for the BBC, gained additional experience both as actor
and producer there. In 1969, when the Bradford Playhouse
and Film Theatre, as it is now called, kept its fortieth anniversary, Peter Dews became president.

The Playhouse gives the public an opportunity to see many
films and live productions which would otherwise never
reach the West Riding. Indeed, it is probably the only
voluntary organization which puts on a play or a film every
week day in the year. If the professional theatre in the
provinces is in jeopardy the Bradford Playhouse, in spite of
all difficulties, is determined to see that the shows go on.

Bradford is often charged with lack of culture, but in one
respect, at least, it is not as black as it is sometimes painted—
it shares the strong choral traditions of the West Riding.

In the early nineteenth century public houses were the
only popular meeting places, and the Bull's Head, Westgate,
where musicians gathered, became the headquarters of the
Old Choral Society, after it left the Market Hall. The Society,
living up to its name, claims to be the second oldest in the
country, with a continuous history from 1820. The Bradford
Festival Choral Society, in 1858, two years after it was
founded, had the distinction of giving three concerts in London, one of them a Command Performance at Buckingham
Palace.

But singing was not regarded as a job only for specialists.
Every place of worship in Bradford had its choir, some of them
very big ones, and it was a poor chapel that couldn't muster
enough members from the neighbourhood to give the *Messiah*
at Christmas.

Bradford's parks have been called its lungs, and it was perhaps with this in mind that each one, even the smallest, was provided with a bandstand. Brass band playing received encouragement from factories and voluntary organizations, notably the Salvation Army, and in the 1930s most parks had two concerts on Sunday, provided, as a rule, by local bands.

The mention of brass bands in Bradford inevitably calls up the "Black Dyke", which for over a century has been associated with Foster's Mill at Queensbury. Queensbury, 1,200ft above sea level, is the highest point on the surrounding hills, and lies just outside the city boundary. John Foster, who founded the mill in 1835, was himself a horn player in the local band, and when its days seemed numbered, he assured its future by making it the firm's own band. Local men who worked at Black Dyke Mills, many of them from Bradford, made this band one of the finest in the world.

The First World War, as the *Bradford Daily Telegraph* said at the time, laid a terribly heavy hand on the city. Most young men were keen to join up, and during the Somme offensive of 1 July 1916 the "Bradford Pals" sustained heavy losses. Night after night women at home searched the lists of killed and missing for names of friends and relatives. Three battalions of the West Yorkshire Regiment which took part in the attack were composed of Bradford men, the "Pals", of whom 2,000 were killed; and this tragedy showed the terrible consequences of drafting men from one neighbourhood into the same fighting unit.

On 21 August, while the casualty lists were still being published in the local paper, one of Bradford's biggest disasters occurred—the Low Moor Explosion. This was at a chemical works, but because of war-time secrecy the official announcement merely reported "an explosion at a munitions factory in Yorkshire". There were, in fact, several detonations, one of which blew up a gasholder, shaking the district for miles around. Thirty-nine people died, and a memorial was placed in Scholemoor Cemetery as a tribute to six firemen who lost their lives in the course of duty.

Low Moor Explosion

Peace did not bring prosperity, and a slump in 1921 left Bradford with 60,000 unemployed. Relief schemes were initiated and it was through one of these that ex-servicemen built the section of Thornton Road which runs over Pitty Beck.

The inter-war years brought serious unemployment and much poverty to northern towns, the period of the General Strike being one of particular distress. It was then, in 1926, that Bradford was thankful for the legacy from disused coal mines in the district. Whole families went out daily for coal in the delphs—the old quarries—around mine workings, and on the many slag heaps.

In 1928 the Low Moor Company, which had survived Bowling Iron Works by thirty years, got into difficulties and closed down, throwing over three thousand employees out of work.

After this trade sank to its lowest level, and in 1939, just when a revival seemed likely, war was declared on Germany. From then on the demand for uniform cloths kept textile workers busy.

In the Second World War Bradford escaped heavy bombardment, but late on the evening of 31 August 1940 there was an air raid in which Rawson Market and the surrounding buildings were hit. Although considerable damage was done casualties were light, and when peace was again restored Bradford was quickly able to resume normal business. In some parts of the country councils were faced with the task of clearing sites of rubble and rebuilding whole town areas. Bradford, by contrast, had to decide upon a vast programme of demolition as part of a project to modernize the over-crowded city centre.

A long-term plan had been prepared by the City Engineer, Mr S. G. Wardley, and at a Civic Exhibition held in Cartwright Hall to celebrate the centenary of the award of the 1847 Charter, a large model of the new central area was displayed. In the City Council, the day of the centenary, 9 June 1947, was commemorated at a special meeting, and the

M

occasion was also marked by the admission of a new Freeman, Sir Edward Appleton, one of Bradford's most distinguished sons.

The celebrations were to have come to a triumphant close in July, with a pageant in Peel Park, but public support was lacking, and because the pageant was badly attended the Corporation sustained a heavy financial loss. The organizers were probably encouraged in their expectations by the Historical Pageant of 1931, but on that occasion the whole of the city's educational resources were brought together with remarkable results.

The Wardley plan, as it now takes shape, contains an inner ring road by means of which through traffic will be dispersed and kept out of the central area. Multi-storey car parks are to be built near every radial road, but roof-level parking sites will actually extend over traffic free shopping precincts. One long-promised improvement, the demolition of the General Post Office, will show off the Cathedral, enhanced by a Close and possibly a Terrace, to great advantage.

The granting of cathedral status in 1920 revealed the limitations of the old church and in 1935 considerable extensions were planned by Sir Edward Maufe. Because of the war, work did not begin until 1951, but then a Song Room was added on the north side of the tower, and a similar extension on the south side provided vestries for the bishop and clergy. The east end of the Cathedral was redesigned and extended, to give an entirely new chancel and three chapels, together with a chapter house. The whole effect is one of spaciousness and light, creating a beauty which belies the somewhat dour and gritty appearance of the old exterior.

In 1965 the Town Hall was renamed the City Hall and a year later the building was thoroughly cleaned to reveal the Cliffe Wood stone in its true colours. When the clock tower was floodlit, many passers-by realized for the first time how handsome the City Hall really was.

The renovation brought interest to bear on a novel feature of the architect's design—a history lesson in stone. In

niches along an "arcade" at third floor level stand the
monarchs of England, from William I onwards, each more
than life size, carved from solid blocks of Bradford stone.
Elizabeth I and Queen Victoria, who stand on either side of the
main entrance, bring the number of statues up to thirty-five.

Since the completion of the original plan there have been
several alterations, giving a new Council Chamber and ban-
queting Hall, and a Civic Staircase. The last alteration, a
three-storey extension, was added in 1963.

In all major improvements to the central area the becks had
to be dealt with first, and on more than one occasion in recent
years deep trenches have been made through the main streets
so that culverts could be strengthened. In spite of all
precautions, serious floods occurred in 1945 and 1946, causing
thousands of pounds worth of damage. But the worst flood
in all Bradford's history took place on an extraordinary
summer day in 1968.

By ten o'clock on the morning of 2 July it became so dark
that people put on their lights. The inevitable storm began
with thunder, lightning and a fury of hail—hail-stones bigger
than marbles—which in turn gave way to torrential rain. The
hailstorm flattened growing plants and stripped trees and
bushes bare: drains and gulleys were choked, and the rain
turned the sloping main streets of Bradford into swift flowing
tributaries, all making for the city centre.

Nearly an inch of rain fell in eight minutes. The city centre
was turned into a lake, and the newly erected subways,
opened only a few weeks before, were flooded to the roof.
Rumour spread that two people were drowned and others
trapped, but frogmen who went to the rescue reported no
casualties. Damage was estimated at £1,000,000, but on the
whole it was agreed that the culverts had withstood the storm
of a century remarkably well.

This event, like all others in the daily life of the city, was
fully reported in Bradford's own evening paper, the *Telegraph
and Argus*, which was a hundred years old that month. The
souvenir edition of the paper, which made special mention of

the flood, showed incredible pictures of Hall Ings covered by a lake, and Canal Road like a river in full spate.

In 1972 work commenced on the construction of a transport interchange in Bridge Street, a costly and ambitious project. Before anything else could be done, however, the Bowling Beck, which ran underneath the site, had to be diverted and a new tunnel made to prevent flooding—an initial expense of £500,000.

Even before one project ended another began, so that as the Law Courts were nearing completion men started to clear the ground for the new Kirkgate Market—all this in the first few months of 1972. In fact, the changes everywhere appeared so drastic that some people said it would have been more sensible to abandon Bradford altogether.

In the suburbs changes were taking place with great rapidity, mainly to make way for new roads. Dudley Hill, once a closely knit little community, no longer exists; and much of old Bowling has already been laid waste, in preparation for the new Manchester Road, with its three-lane dual carriage ways. Whatever else, the planners are determined that Bradford shall not be "on a siding" as far as road transport is concerned. The completion of the South Bradford M606, which follows a similar route to the proposed through railway line past Oakenshaw, means that drivers will be able to travel to London entirely by motorway.

One item of good news concerns Low Moor, which never recovered after the closure of the iron works. Here the north's biggest international freight terminal is to be built. The choice of Bradford, in preference to Manchester was, it is said, greatly helped by its shipping agents, who have made a reputation for themselves as experts in container traffic. It was felt, too, that Bradford would be in a better position to deal with Common Market countries through the east coast ports.

In areas scheduled for redevelopment Bradford has lost many historic and interesting buildings which were part of its tradition. One by one the old halls have gone, too.

Horton Hall, the home of the Parliamentarian branch of the Sharp family, after being used as a bishop's residence until 1955, fell into disrepair and was demolished. There is no memorial here, but a plaque on the wall of Martin's Bank, Ivegate, marks the site of the home of John Sharp, a relative who became Archbishop of York. This house was also used by General Fairfax as his headquarters during the Civil War.

Bierley Hall was so badly damaged by vandals after 1968 that it, too, had to be demolished. Paper Hall in Church Bank, a much smaller residence dating from 1648, was still standing in the early 1970s and a belated attempt was being made to save it.

Bolling Hall, one of the district's most interesting historic houses, is fortunate to survive. In 1816, the owner, Sir Francis Lindley Wood, sold the estate to the Bowling Iron Company, after which the hall was occupied by various tenants. Towards the end of the nineteenth century it was divided into tenements and became neglected. By good chance, in 1912, Mr G. A. Paley made a timely gift of the hall to Bradford Corporation, who converted it into a domestic museum.

The oldest part of the hall is the fifteenth century tower, through which visitors enter, but additions to the building have been made at all periods since that date. The "Ghost Room", where the Earl of Newcastle slept, is a notable attraction, but the main room, the "Housebody", is of special interest. The large window here contains valuable stained glass in the form of twenty-four heraldic shields, including those of the Bolling and Tempest families. The old market cross in the grounds will eventually find a permanent place in the new Kirkgate Market.

Royds Hall, Low Moor, provides one of the most pleasant surprises. Here, at the end of an unmade road, high on a hill overlooking an expanse of country bounded by the Pennines, stands the old home of the Rookes family. When the Low Moor Company was formed Royds Hall was occupied first by Joseph Dawson and then by other partners. It is good to report that the old manor hall is now a well preserved private residence.

The sudden realization that many irreplaceable relics of Bradford's more recent history were quickly disappearing led to a decision by the Council to create an industrial museum. Accordingly, at Moorside Mills, Eccleshill, exhibits of all kinds have been assembled and large pieces of machinery erected to form a valuable extension of the museums service, which stems from Cartwright Hall.

During the boom years of the nineteenth century there seemed no reason why "Bradford worsted", like "Best York-shire" iron, should not go on for ever. But steel ousted cast iron, and man-made fibres have challenged the supremacy of wool. A revolution in business methods has rendered the Exchange, so vital when it was founded, almost unnecessary today.

Wool textiles are still the major industry in Bradford and district, but in 1970 mills were reported to be closing at the rate of one a week. Many firms who were once household names have now either gone out of business or been taken over by combines. But it is a mistake to under-estimate the variety of Bradford's manufactures, which absorb, among other things, a very large part of the world's crops of alpaca, mohair and cashmere. Outside textiles there have been many developments, especially in engineering and light industries, so that girls who would once have "gone into t'mill", almost as a matter of course, may now start work on a television assembly line, or at one of the two largest mail order firms in the country.

The all-importance of wool to Bradford has often drawn attention from interesting ventures in other fields. Tractors, for instance, are made on premises at Idle which formerly turned out a team of well-known Jowett cars. The high speed Jowett *Jupiter* broke the course record and gained the class award at Le Mans in 1950 and in the following year won its class at the Monte Carlo Rally. The 1½ litre *Javelin* saloon

gained many international honours, while the Jowett range
of vans was naturally very popular at home. When the out-
fall tunnel at Esholt Sewage Works was completed a convoy
of Jowett cars was proudly driven through it—a gesture
obviously intended to illustrate the spirit of local enterprise.

Jupiter at Le Mans

A Victorian visitor to Bradford, reflecting on all the
changes and pondering the future of the Wool Exchange,
would no doubt have memories revived by the much enlarged
neighbouring store of Brown Muff's.

Henry Brown inherited his mother's draper's shop, near
the Hope and Anchor Inn on Market Street, and took his
brother-in-law, Mr Muff, into partnership with him. Brown
Muff's, which dates from 1814, is still a family concern and
very much part of the city. Alderman Brown, three times
Mayor of Bradford, was a staunch, well respected figure in
both commercial and public life, and students who gain
"Henry Brown" awards benefit from his generous bequests to
educational trusts.

Our visitor would also be impressed by the change in Bradford's population. Even fifty years ago the sight of a "black
man" in the streets was enough to make children stand and
stare or run away. Now the city is almost as renowned for its
immigrants as for its wool.

By "immigrants" we usually mean people from Asia or the

West Indies, but the first batch of settlers were mainly Poles and Ukrainians, fourteen thousand of whom came to Bradford from Displaced Persons Camps in Germany after 1945. Three years later small numbers of West Indians began to arrive, and in 1951 promise of work brought in men from India and Pakistan.

The main employment for the newcomers was in wool-combing, especially on the night turn, where the heat and unpleasant conditions had created a labour shortage. The city's buses were short-staffed, too, and before long posters in Urdu were inviting applications from men wishing to train as conductors or drivers. By 1964 immigrants comprised a third of all the bus crews.

The aim of these men at first was to send money home to support their families, but by degrees wives, children and more distant relatives joined them here. They settled in depressed areas, in back-to-backs or terrace houses where several families could live together and share the rent. In Lumb Lane and the surrounding district, shops and cafes with foreign names soon sprang up. Before long one Asian had become the landlord of a pub and others, no less enterprising, opened estate agencies and driving schools. Religion played a large part in their lives, so that by 1971 Bradford had three mosques and two Sikh temples.

The educational services in particular were strained by the continuing influx of immigrant children, amounting at the peak period to one new class each week. The local authority adopted a policy whereby, in an attempt to spread the burden, pupils were sent to schools in outlying districts when numbers in nearby schools were too high. Registers were soon sprinkled with unpronounceable names from the East and romantic names like Nathaniel Parchment Hilton from the West. Traditional letters to teacher were enlivened by others starting, "Good morning Miss", or, "Dear Sir, I most humbly and respectfully beg you to grant Hussain live for one day." Happily, children erect few barriers, and neither creed nor colour prevented friendships from being quickly established.

General estimates of immigrant numbers vary greatly, 20,000 being an average figure. But school returns, which are accurate, say there were over 7,000 of these children in Bradford schools in 1972 including, of course, many who were born in the city. Much has already been done, but with this proportion still showing signs of increase, the integration of a mixed population may present one of the biggest problems in the history of "the friendly city".

We have been following the progress of Bradford, from a nameless settlement to the centre of the world's wool industry, but on 1 April 1974 its history as an independent city will come to an end. On that date, under plans for local government reform, Bradford is to take its place with nine other townships as a member of District 6A in the West Yorkshire Metropolitan County Area. The ten councils, among which are Keighley, Ilkley and Shipley, will combine to shape future policy and establish new traditions. Already the new authority has decided to apply for city status and a coat of arms.

This change is seen by some as Bradford's chance to emerge from its isolation in a cul-de-sac off the Aire Valley and become a leading member of a new Dales community; for if Bradford is not, like Skipton, the "Gateway to the Dales", it is a very good starting point.

Bradfordians have always had a great fondness for Wharfedale, the pride and joy of the West Riding. They speak of the Cow and Calf Rocks with affection and sing "On Ilkla Moor baht 'at" as though it were their own anthem. While there is no intention of creating a "Bigger Bradford" nothing would seem more natural than a partnership with Ilkley.

In Airedale, Bradford has often cast covetous eyes on Shipley, which includes Saltaire, but amalgamation has always been resisted. Now, without annexation, the union is to take place. With Keighley, Bradford will play a major role in the industrial affairs of the new district. Very little has been made of the fact that four of the Bronte children were born at

View across to City Hall from New Library

Thornton, but Bradford people are very proud of their association with the Brontes. Haworth will come with Keighley into the new district; thus the beginning and the end of the Bronte story will be brought, so to speak, under one roof.

Bradford's prestige was raised in 1966 when a long cherished ambition was fulfilled. The University, which began life as the Institute of Technology, was granted its Charter in that year, and the then Prime Minister, the Rt Hon Harold Wilson, became the first Chancellor. While rapid development continues at the University a large extension is planned for the Technical College nearby, in a scheme which includes a new Regional College of Art.

Now, with an expanding University; a fine Central Library; a Cathedral shortly to be enhanced by a new setting; a modern city centre, and with opportunities in so many industrial fields, Bradford, "the town on a siding", bids fair to become the place where all roads meet.

INDEX

Adwalton Moor, 59–60, 63
Aire, River, 11–13, 17, 19–20,
    24–5, 27, 46, 63, 74, 83, 125–6,
    144, 171, 185
Alhambra, 173
Alpaca, 142–3, 146, 148, 182
Althorp Act (1833), 109–10
Angora, 134
Anglo-Saxons, 16, 18–21
Appleton, Sir E., 178
Apperley Viaduct, 125–7
Ashley, (Shaftesbury) Lord, 105, 109,
    156

Back-to-backs, 135, 170
Baildon, 12, 13, 46
Balme, Abraham, 76
Balme, Matthew, 156
Behrens, Sir J., 118, 158
Bierley, 17, 20, 48, 55, 75
Bierley Hall, 17, 181
Bingley, 17, 20, 48, 55, 75
Black Dyke Mills, 175
Blaize Festival, 93–7, 141
Boar Legend, 39–40, 134
Bolling family, 43, 181
Bolling Hall, 42, 43, 100–1, 79, 96,
    110, 156, 181
Bowling, 23, 28, 30, 84, 118, 147–8,
    180
Bowling Ironworks, 76, 85–6, 112,
    156, 177, 181
Boyce, Thomas, 173
BRADFORD
  Beck, 11–12, 20, 32, 34, 45, 77–9,
    83–4, 179
  Canal, 74–7, 119, 124–5, 133
  Charter, (1847), 42, 132–41, 144,
    177
  Central Library, 188
  Coat of Arms, 39, 134, 185
  Education Committee, 167–8
  Exhibition, (1904), 170–1
  Festival Choral Society, 174
  Fulling mill, 32–3, 36–8, 48
  Girls' Grammar School, 159
  Grammar School, 157–9, 161
  High School, 158
  Manor Hall, 32–4, 79, 136, 137,
    173
  Mayors, 133–4, 144
  Mechanics' Institute, 160–3
  MPs, 63, 120, 137, 147, 157, 159
  Parish Church, (Cathedral), 20–1,
    29–30, 33, 36, 43–4, 54–5, 58,
    61, 63, 70–1, 80, 96, 127, 134,
    137, 155
  Piece Hall, 72, 76, 79, 117
  Playhouse, 173
  Population, 23, 36–7, 78, 93, 132,
    155, 183, 162, 170
  School Board, 162–6, 169
  Corn Mill, 32–40, 98, 169
  Technical College, 131, 160–1,
    188
  Telegraph & Argus, 134, 179–80
  Town (City) Hall, 32, 139, 147,
    149, 178
  University, 188
Bridge Street, 12, 61, 70, 128, 156,
    180
Brigantes, 15–16, 22
Brontes, 185–8
Broad ford, 20, 23
Bronze Age, 12, 14, 22, 46
Brown, Henry, 183
Bull, Rev. G. S., 101, 103, 104–5,
    107–9, 114, 154, 156
Bussey, Peter, 115

Canals, 72–7, 119, 124
Carding, 68, 82
Cartwright Memorial Hall, 14, 46,
    151, 170, 181
Cartwright, Rev. E., 90–2, 119–20,
    122
Celts, 14–15, 18–19
Charles I, 36, 49, 51–2, 64
Charles II, 63
Chartists, 115, 153–4
Chellow Dene, 12, 23
Chellow Heights, 13

189

Christ Church, 154
Church Bank, 20, 58, 78, 91
Church, Esmé, 174
Church Schools, 154, 159, 162
Civil War, 51, 65, 97
Cliffe Wood, 39–40, 42, 87, 134
Clitheroe, 25, 28
Coal, 76, 82, 85–6, 177
Cockpit Building, 79
Cobden, Richard, 139
Combing machines, 92–3, 119–23, 131
Corker, Rev. F., 64
Court House, 114–15, 134, 139, 159
Cranbrook, Lord, 137
Crosse, Rev. J., 81
Cuckoo Bridge, 32
Cup-and-ring stones, 13–14, 22

Danes, 21, 23, 44
Dawson, Rev. J., 86, 181
Defoe, Daniel, 67, 132
Deira, 19–22
de Lacys, 22–35
Delius, Frederick, 118
Delius, Julius, 118
Dewes, Peter, 174
Dewsbury, 19
District 6A, 185
Domesday Book, 20, 22–3, 25, 31
Donisthorpe, G. E., 121, 131
Donskoi, 142
Dudley Hill, 17, 180

Eccleshill, 18, 23
Education Act 1870, 159–61, 165
Edward I, 30, 34
Edward II, 35–6
Edward III, 35–6, 46–9, 96
Edward IV, 43, 45
Elmet, 16, 19
Emmett's Foundry, 85–6
Endowed Schools Act 1869, 157–9
Esholt, 170–2, 183
Extent 1342, 35, 37–8, 40, 48

Factory Acts, 109–10
Factory children, 93, 101–13, 162
Fairfax, Lord Ferdinando, 53, 59, 61
Fairfax, Sir Thomas, 53–4, 59–63, 181
Farnley Wood Plot, 64
Fawcett, Rev. J., 77, 113
Fawcett, Richard, 42, 93, 96–7
Flemish weavers, 49, 67
Floods, 84, 179
Forster, W. E., 113, 152–62
Fountains Abbey, 22, 47
Frizinghall, 48

Gamel, 22, 24, 26
Garnett, James, 91, 145
Garnett's Mill, 108
Gaunt, John of, 27, 36, 41
George III, 87
German merchants, 70, 117–19
Ghant, Alice de, 27
Goit Side, 83, 135–6
Great Exhibition, 1851, 130–1

Hall Ings, 27, 70, 180
Hand-combers, 98–9, 122–3
Hanson, James, 162–3
Hardy, John, 86, 120, 137
Hartley, James, 39, 72, 74, 76–7
Haworth, 19, 23, 38, 44, 114, 188
Heap, Rev. H., 97, 155
Henry, Earl of Derby, 35–6
Henry I, 27
Henry III, 29
Henry IV, 36
Henry VII, 31
Henry VIII, 44, 171
Hinsley, Cardinal, 164
Hodgson, Capt. J., 54
Holme, The, 92, 94, 96, 141
Horsfalls' Mill, 99–100
Horton, 23, 28, 31–2, 36, 40–2, 48, 79, 80–1, 84, 91, 94, 96
Horton Hall, 51, 101, 181
Hudson, Geoffrey, 125
Hustler, John, 69–75
Hunt Yard, 40, 42, 94

Idle, 17, 23, 85, 114, 171, 182
Ilkley, 12, 13, 16, 17, 19, 21, 185
Independent Labour Party, 149–50, 165
Industrial Museum, 181
Industrial Revolution, 69, 82, 83–4, 90–100
Inquisition, 1277, 30–1
Inquisition, 1311, 32, 38
Immigrants, 103–5, 135, 159
Iron Age, 15
Irving, Sir Henry, 173
Ivegate, 17, 33, 43, 78, 87, 96

James, John, 11, 23, 32, 34, 113
Jowett Cars, 182–3
Jowett, Fred, 151, 165

Keighley, 69, 74, 185
Keeling, Rev. W. H., 158
Kerr, Dr. J., 165–6
Kirkgate, 20, 33, 55, 70, 72, 77–8, 84, 96, 126, 137
Kirkgate Market, 137, 180, 181
Kirkstall Abbey, 27–8, 32, 44, 47, 48

Lancaster, Thomas, Earl of, 34–5
Leaventhorpe, 21–2
Leeds–Bradford Railway, 123–7
Leeds–Liverpool Canal, 74–6, 125
Leland, John, 44–5, 83
Lister, E. C., 120
Lister, J. C., 120
Lister, Joseph, 51–62, 158
Lister, S. C. (Baron Masham), 120, 148–51, 161, 170
Lister's Mill, 120–1, 149, 151, 170–1
Lister's Strike, 149
Low Moor Company, 76, 82, 85–7, 112–13, 115, 137, 177, 181
Low Moor Day School, 86, 113, 156
Low Moor Explosion, 175
Luddism, 92, 99–100, 116

MacArthur, Capt. J., 88
McMillan, Margaret, 164–8
McMillan, Rachel, 164, 167
Maufe, Sir E., 178
Manningham, 20, 23, 36, 38, 40
Manningham (Lister) Park, 141, 151, 160–1, 170, 172
Manningham, Roger de, 41
Market Hall, (old) 72, 79, 154–5, 174
Market Street, 79, 84, 96
Markets, 29–33, 36, 79, 87, 137
Marsden, Rev. S., 87–9, 120, 122

Newcastle, Earl of, 54, 59, 60–2
Nidd Valley Scheme, 137, 169
Noble, John, 122
Norfolk, 49, 67
Normans, 22–37, 47
Northrop, John de, 40
Northumbria, 19, 21
Norwich, 67–8, 74

Oastler, Richard, 101–3, 109–10, 114, 156, 161, 165
O'Connor, Rev. (Monsignor) J., 164
Octagon Chapel, 79
Old Choral Society, 174
Old Exchange, 152

Pack horses, 48, 69, 74
Paper Hall, 91, 99, 181
Paulinus, 19
Peckover, Edmund, 75, 98
Peel, Sir Robert, 161, 169
Peel Park, 146–7, 169, 178
Picts & Scots, 16, 18
Pieceners, 109
Place-names, 19–22
Plug drawing riots, 115–16
Poll Tax, 1379, 33, 36–7, 49
Pontefract, 24, 29, 32, 35, 37, 41, 59

Poor Law Act, 1834, 113–14, 135
Poor Law Riots, 113–15
Power, Alfred, 108, 114
Power looms, 91, 93, 116, 119
Priestley, Jonathan, 168
Priestley, J. B. 168, 173

Quakers, 70, 75, 153
Quarries, 87, 120, 151, 169–70

Railways, 85, 117, 130–1, 156, 171
Ramsbotham, Robert, 91–2, 120
Rawson Market, 137, 177
Rawson, William, 72, 79, 137
Richard I, 28, 47
Richard II, 36–7
Richardson, Dr Richard, 17, 158
Ripley, George, 118, 147
Ripley, (Sir) H., 147–8, 159
Roebuck Inn, 115, 135
Rombalds Moor, 12, 13
Romans, 15–19
Royds Hall, 85–6, 181

Sadler Committee, 103–5
Sadler, Michael, 102–4, 109
St George's Hall, 139, 146, 149, 160, 169
St Mary's Chapel, 135
St Sitha, 44
Salt, Sir Titus, 131, 142–8, 157, 163
Saltaire, 48, 131, 139, 142–7, 185
Scar House Reservoir, 136
Schools:
    Bowling Back Lane, 162
    Feversham Street, 163
    Green Lane, 168
    St Ann's 164
    St Bede's, 164
    Wapping, 162, 166
Schuster, Leo, 118
Scoresby, Dr. W., 155–6
Selby Abbey, 27
Sharp, John (Archbishop of York), 157, 181
— John, 51, 62
— Thomas, 28
— Abraham, 157
Shipley, 46, 83, 93, 145
Short Time Committees, 102, 110
Silk, 148–9
Spinning, 46, 49, 69–72, 82, 90–2, 105–10
Spur tenure, 28, 32–3
Stansfield, 171
Stephenson, George, 125
Stephenson, Robert, 125
Stone, 76, 82, 87

Stone heads, 14–15
Sunday Schools, 79, 104, 107, 154–5

Tanning, 45–6
Tempest, Richard, 43, 60, 181
Ten Hours Bill, 102–3, 105, 110, 156
Tentering, 37–8
Theatre Royal, 173
Thompson, Ald. M. W., 141
Thompson's Mill, 136
Thornton, 13, 23, 83, 188
Tong, 23, 44, 87, 114
Tong Street, 17–18
Tonnington, Robert, 30
Turles, 32, 79
Transport, 72–8, 121–32, 171, 172, 178, 180
Turnpike roads, 74, 119, 124

Undercliffe, 53, 65, 70

Vikings, 21–2
Volunteers, 71, 92

Wakefield, 37, 44, 59, 74, 117
Walkers, (fullers), 37–8, 48
Watchmen, 80–1
Water supply, 81–2, 83–5, 136–7, 169
Waterhouse, Rev. J., 64

Wardley, S. G., 177–8
Waud, C. & Co., 139, 144
Weaving, 46–9, 67–9, 70–2, 78, 91–4, 97–9, 116, 119, 132
Wesley, John, 79
Westgate, 17, 33, 38, 55, 79, 87, 136, 154
Wharfe, River, 13, 19
White Lion Inn, 70
Whitelaw, Billie, 174
Wibsey, 23–4, 28, 85
William I, 22–6
William II, 26
Windhill, 75–6
Wood, Sir F. L., 181
Wood, John, 101, 103, 105, 108, 156
Wood's Mill, 104–5, 109–10, 156
Wood's School, 108, 156
Wool (export), 47–8
Wool Exchange, 72, 96, 139, 182
Woolcombers' Aid Association, 122–3
Woolcombing, 67–70, 97–9, 116, 121–3
Woollen, 67–8
Woolsacks, 47, 54, 61, 134
Worsted, 67–8,
Wright, Dr. Joseph, 163

York, 16, 17, 21, 25, 29, 46, 48, 49, 59, 64, 82
Yorkists, 43